The Complete Hiking Guide to Zion National Park

Eleven Easy-to-Hard Trails for Adventure Seekers Exploring Utah

VERA FULLER

TABLE OF CONTENTS

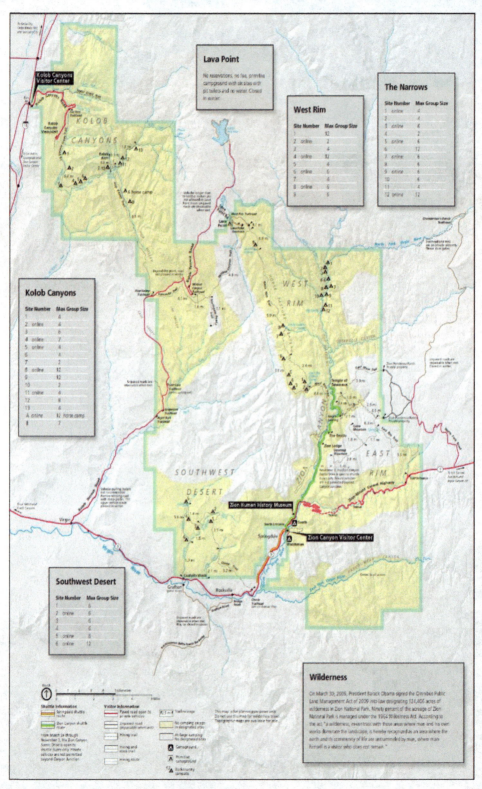

Lava Point

No reservations, no fee, primitive campground with six sites with pit toilets and no water. Closed in winter.

West Rim

Site Number	Max Group Size
1	12
2 online	2
3	4
4 online	12
5	4
6 online	6
7	4
8 online	6
9	6

The Narrows

Site Number	Max Group Size
1 online	4
2	4
3 online	6
4	2
5 online	6
6	12
7 online	6
8	6
9 online	6
10	4
11	4
12 online	12

Kolob Canyons

Site Number	Max Group Size
1	4
2 online	4
3	6
4 online	7
5 online	4
6	6
7	2
8 online	12
9	12
10	2
11 online	6
12	8
13	6
A online	12 horse camp
B	7

Southwest Desert

Site Number	Max Group Size
1	6
2 online	6
3	6
4 online	6
5 online	6
6 online	12

Wilderness

On March 30, 2009, President Barack Obama signed the Omnibus Public Land Management Act of 2009 into law designating 124,406 acres of wilderness in Zion National Park. Ninety percent of the acreage of Zion National Park is managed under the 1964 Wilderness Act. According to the act "a wilderness, in contrast with those areas where man and his own works dominate the landscape, is hereby recognized as an area where the earth and its community of life are untrammeled by man, where man himself is a visitor who does not remain."

INTRODUCTION

A few years back, I was hiking with my four girls. It was a sunny day, one of our first hikes of the summer season. I recently bought all five matching windbreakers for us. We felt fierce on the trail; everyone noticed our braided hair and matching pink jackets.

We hiked along with not a care in the world. That is when we got to the tricky part of the hike. You have to walk upstream to reach the canyon! I knew my girls were up for it since they have had experience with many stream crossings.

Still, the river was muddy and full of algae. Nevertheless, my group decided this won't be a problem for us. We all took each other's hands, opened the belt straps on our backpacks, and fearlessly started walking through the water.

A few steps forward, and that was when I felt it. My leg was touching something slimy. Later I found out it was the local cyanobacteria algae. My leg slipped, and I could feel my whole body slowly shifting to the back. Instead of letting my hand go, my girls were brave and held onto me.

I SCREAMED! Sadly, they weren't strong enough to keep my balance for me, and I quickly ended up in the water.

I found my balance again and stopped a few feet downriver. That was when I heard the whole trail, packed full of people, laughing at me, together with my girls, who were all safe on the other side of the river. In fact, the people there weren't even laughing at me. They were laughing with me! I was embarrassed but still managed to see the positive in this situation.

Once I got back onto my feet, I could only think about sharing this experience with everyone so they could laugh with me. I still laugh to this day thinking about that experience, and it's a great conversation starter. Zion National Park was the exact location this anecdote took place, and the Narrows on the Virgin River was the river hike I failed so horribly.

I saw then how nature, like any mother, never ceases to remind us of who we are and humbles us, even when we think we are unstoppable. It makes me think back to when hiking and camping were my wishes. I am sure you know how it feels too!

I remember back in the day when my family and I were just starting out with hiking. We didn't know where to start. It was an actual mess! There were no free resources, trails weren't well maintained, and information about campsites was scarce.

For most people starting today and wanting to take themselves, their partners, or their family to see any national park, this might also seem like a huge problem. You don't know where to look for information, where to find campsites, and what trails to choose. Truth be said, today, it is much easier to access any kind of information, but it is anything but easy.

You need to know where to look. You have to combine blog reviews, official sites, and tour guides to get to the middle ground and figure out what is true and what isn't. That is where I come in. But more on me later.

Not knowing where to start and where to look is why you sit at home, looking at pictures of landscapes and wishing you could spend your vacation in the wild instead of Disneyland. Your soul yearns for the wilderness, views, sunsets, and privacy. I know you are facing the same problems I once had. That is why I am here to help you!

I was once like you too! My husband worked in a big oil company and was rarely home. I was caring for the kids and looking for ways to find a side buck. Sadly, we were part of the "grind culture." One day, we just stopped taking part in it.

We took a long vacation in a local park, started hiking and fishing, and spent our nights in the tent. This was when it all began. It was so liberating. Finally, be what we truly are! And I know if I can do it, you can do it too!

This book will show you what you were missing out on, and since you will read it in one breath (I am sure of it), it will give you an extra push into the wild. Once you have all the information you need, you will feel like you have wings. You will finally be ready to fly, and by fly, I mean hike!

That is how I felt once I slipped and ended up in the Virgin River at the Narrows. I laughed at myself, unable to start and not thinking I was ready. You, your partner, and your family are prepared to spend time outdoors because the outdoors is for everyone!

We need to revel in this beauty and explore our surroundings first. Only then should we see the rest of the world. That is why this book right here will tell you all you need to know about Zion National Park and teach you how to marvel at its beauty.

This book offers you a glimpse into what you need to know about the park, its background, history, hikes, formation, and natural life. But more importantly, it offers a list of shortcuts for each reader, which will minimize your research process and tell each person where they can camp, what trails to take, what to pay attention to, and any possible hazards.

It might sound too good to be true, but it is true! Finally, a complete guide that won't need any additional reading! Soon, you and your family will have a campsite with a sunset view and a fire to make yourselves a tasty dinner. All will be well.

Now, why am I here, and who am I to share this information with you? I am Vera Fuller, a mother of four (above-mentioned) wild girls. Apart from being a massive fan of Zion National Park, I am a seasoned hiker with numerous years of hiking, camping, and trekking under my belt.

Being part of a group that enjoys nature or spending time solo in nature is good for the soul. That is why I have so far spent most of my free time in the wilderness. That always includes my family. For you, it can just be you and your dog, a group of friends, or your partner. You decide.

I sure wish I had this book while starting out with my camping experiences! That was almost ten years ago, and since then, I have learned a lot about other parks individually. Every time I visit, I see a new side of Zion too. That is why I am here to help you and make learning easier. To push you and seal the deal on your camping and hiking adventure.

As you might expect, accumulating all this knowledge took a long time, so this is why I am the right person to write this book. I love taking my little family hiking or just a simple weekend getaway with my husband to enjoy the outdoors. Many people have noticed my fire for nature and asked when I'll write a book or do a podcast because they would love to know my thoughts.

That is why this book is here for you. It can help both beginners and intermediate hikers get to know the trails and knowledgeable hikers visiting Zion National Park for the first time.

I understand that many people here think of national parks as barren stretches of land. On the contrary! If you are ready to learn about Zion National Park, keep reading. I will show you the natural wonders and awe-inspiring trails, so you can know what this park is all about.

ZION NATIONAL PARK

The United States has over 60 national parks! Now imagine this since each has unique characteristics, natural wonders, and cultural significance; they are protected by the National Park Service, a federal agency that oversees the preservation and management of these areas.

These are some of the world's most stunning and iconic national parks. While all national parks are worth visiting, Zion National Park stands out. Now, let's see why!

This national park lies in southwestern Utah in the United States of America. Most of the public knows it by its breathtaking cliffs, blushing desert, and narrow canyons. Zion truly is all those things but also scenic hikes, rock columns, and red sunsets.

A long time ago, people couldn't believe this type of landscape could stand on the face of the Earth. That was when few people visited the park.

Zion Canyon is at the heart of the park, carved through the force of water for millennia. It is a steep-walled gorge formed by the Virgin River, which flows through the park's center. Apart from providing a lifeline for the park's plant and animal life, it was initially named Mukuntuweap or "Straight Canyon."

It was first established as Mukuntuweap National Monument in 1909. As Mukuntuweap, it only had around 300 visitors, so the administration blamed the name for its low popularity.

In 1919 it was later designated as Zion National Park, Utah's first national park. Since the name change, it has become one of the most visited parks in the US, with millions of visitors each year.

This canyon, national monument, and now a national park are ever-changing. Natural forces constantly carve its vast area of 229 square miles. That makes Zion National Park unique, so tourists keep visiting it repeatedly.

All these elements make Zion a popular destination for hikers, climbers, and nature lovers worldwide. Their main goal is to experience dramatic landscapes, wild waters, steep rock faces, and unique geology.

Thanks to the river and its currents, visitors can enjoy various activities ranging from scenic drives and short hikes to multi-day backpacking trips and rock-climbing adventures.

As you will later see, a Mormon that settled here had named the area Little Zion. In the Bible, Zion is a place of refuge. Truly, Zion Park is a place of refuge in nature. Now, I will show you how this magnificent area came to be, from its geological background to its first settlers, and finally, I will tell you what this area is known for today.

You will see why this park is a must-visit destination. That goes for anyone who loves the great outdoors. That includes you too, regardless of if you are a beginner hiker or a seasoned pro. Zion welcomes everyone and shows off what it has to offer.

History Of Mukuntuweap

Zion National Park might seem inhabitable and barren, but it proves man can live in collaboration with nature. The park has a rich history of human habitation, which dates back to thousands of years. The park area was once called home by several Native American tribes. They include the Paiute, Hopi, Navajo, and Anasazi.

The Paiute people were the primary inhabitants of the Zion area, and they were the first to name the park "Mukuntuweap." They lived in harmony with nature for thousands of years before the arrival of the first Europeans.

These people lived a nomadic lifestyle, moving with herds of wild animals. Their lifestyle took advantage of food sources such as pine nuts, game animals, and fish. They formed a deep spiritual connection to the land and believed in their creator, Coyote.

Another culture that formed Zion National Park as we know it today was the Anasazi people. They are best known for their elaborate cliff dwellings, which can be found throughout the Zion area.

The Anasazi were more than just skilled farmers, growing crops such as maize, beans, and squash. They were a society that lived in large, multi-story buildings made of stone, adobe, and wood and was known for their advanced knowledge of architecture, astronomy, and mathematics.

Like most Native Americans, this culture also had a rich spiritual life, and their beliefs were closely tied to the natural world. Some experts believe drought, food shortages, and conflict with neighboring tribes may have contributed to their decline.

That is why the Paiute took over Zion. In the late 1800s, European settlers began to move into the Zion area. Constant conflicts arose between the natives and the newcomers. After years of fighting, the Mukuntuweap Canyon was taken over by new settlers, most of them Mormons.

In 1872, after exploring the Colorado River, John Wesley Powell, an American geologist, traveled to other canyons, visiting the gorge of the North Fork, and writing its name down as Mukuntuweap. That was the first time the name was written down as the Native American term for "Straight Canyon."

Soon, the world will also learn of the glory of (what we know today as) Zion. Nearly 30 years later, artist Frederick Dellenbaugh joined one of Powell's trips. That is when he spent a summer painting in Zion Canyon.

A few years later, he showed his paintings at St. Louis World's Fair and wrote an article about this experience. He wrote down that the visitors at the exhibition thought his paintings were a product of his imagination. Only when a local Mormon convinced them otherwise did the frenzy of wanting to know more about Zion start. While promoting the soon-to-be national park, the author stated: *There is almost nothing to compare to it.*

Mormon pioneers, who settled in the nearby town of Springdale, began to explore the area, and established several small settlements in the canyon. These were the first settlers inside today's national park. Still, this does not minimize the influence the Native Americans had on the area. On the contrary, they were the first to explore, settle, and name the local area.

The tribes that once called this desert their home knew how important Mukuntuweap was and still is. They came here to live, hunt, and socialize. It was a cornerstone for people back in the day. Even today, this value is amplified by naming Zion a national park.

Named A National Park

In 1861, Isaac Behunin was the first to live and cultivate land downriver from the Zion Canyon Valley. He will soon become the most important inhabitant of the Zion National Park area. Behunin gave his new home the name "Zion." Just like the tribes, other settlers came and established their homes here.

In 1909, President William Howard Taft designated the area as a national monument. The name of the newly established monument was Mukuntuweap National Monument. One can see why the locals wanted it changed since it was hard to read, write, and pronounce.

We know precisely who it was that thought so. After visiting the national monument in 1917, Horace Albright, the acting director of the Park Service, believed he knew one of the reasons why people did not see the area. He thought the park's original name needed to be clearer to pronounce and spell.

The name "Mukuntuweap" describes the steep-walled canyon that runs through the heart of the park. In other words, we today know it as Zion Canyon. Isaac Behunin was, therefore, the person who gave Zion its new name.

The park was renamed Zion National Park in 1919 by an act of Congress and President Woodrow Wilson. Luckily, Congress didn't just throw away the old name of the area. It expanded the protected territory too. Locals who used it suggested this new name for the canyon.

They truly believed that the area was a sanctuary, much like the biblical city of Zion. In fact, many people at the time thought so too. One of them was Albright, Parks Service Director, who, as mentioned above, soon thought of Zion as one of his favorite sites. Once you decide to visit, you will be convinced too, as was I when I first saw these amazing rock towers.

During the early years of the park, development couldn't have been faster. That was due to its remote location and rugged terrain.

Local senators and government officials had the first road up the canyon completed in 1917. Initially, visitors would take buses from Cedar City, Utah, to the park, and everything else followed, including the construction of Zion Lodge in 1925.

Between 1927 and 1930, the administration undertook one of the most impressive construction projects in Zion National Park. It involved the blasting of a 1.1-mile tunnel through solid sandstone. This road connected Zion's east side with Mt. Carmel. The tunnel featured lookout "galleries," which were cut like windows into the rock to provide visitors with a better view of the canyon below.

Several hiking trails were also constructed during that time, including the renowned "Walter's Wiggles" section on the way up to Angel's Landing. In 1937, Kolob Canyon was designated a national monument and soon incorporated into Zion National Park.

Today, Zion National Park is one of the most popular national parks in the country. It boasts millions of visitors each year. It is known for its dramatic landscapes, including the towering sandstone cliffs of Zion Canyon, the emerald pools and waterfalls of the Virgin River, and the narrow slot canyons of the park's backcountry.

Zion Today

Since the first year of tracking visitor numbers, tourists have been on the rise. So much so that park officials plan to participate in a reservation system. This aimed to limit the number of visitors and protect the soil from erosion and animal and plant life.

Still, this should not keep you from visiting. Remember, Zion is there to host everyone, even though we might need to wait longer. Therefore, let this be a sign to start planning your Zion trip today, even if this might be your first camping trip. Don't let it scare you; enjoy the uncertainty in a new adventure.

That being said, you do need to know that flash floods can occur. It is primarily during monsoon season but can happen every other season after heavy rainfall too. Therefore, follow the park's regulations or ask rangers about the situation of the trail. Most importantly, stay alert and expect anything from mid-July to September.

In addition to this, you will also need to plan your stays because huge crowds are familiar here. Weekends and holidays like Easter, Independence Day, Memorial Day, and Labor Day are the busiest times. Therefore, I recommend you plan accordingly and make reservations in advance.

But when is the best time to visit Zion National Park? If you ask me, every month is an excellent time to visit Zion. Still, the park is most enjoyable between April and November.

Why? Because this is when the park's shuttle service is available, and the weather is mild. I use April and November to visit due to the thinner crowds and pleasant weather. This is when the average daytime temperatures are comfortable too.

On the other hand, the period between May and September is the high season. Additionally, temperatures during this period can soar, but the temperatures aren't the only thing high. No, the accommodation prices and shuttle wait times will rise too, not to mention the number of visitors and crowds.

Mid-July to September is Zion's monsoon season, so ensure you are prepared for rainfall. I also enjoy the low season. There are fewer visitors between December and February, but some popular attractions, like the Narrows and Angels Landing, could be closed due to bad weather.

While snowfall is not a big issue in the canyon, the months between December and February will be icy. The free shuttle service is unavailable during this time, so you must rely on your own car. Still, you can be sure there will be fewer crowds and lower hotel rates.

Even though we might love it with all our hearts, Zion is slowly fading away. The lines to enter the park, board shuttles, and find parking are becoming longer every season. That is only part of it since campgrounds and trails are deteriorating faster with more visitors.

Funding is also short, with constant damage to vegetation and wildlife. That is why Zion National Park needs to limit the number of visitors in the park.

Geology Of the Straight Canyon

We are all part of something bigger. The same goes for our national parks. None of them are excluded from the local geography or geology. No, they are all part of a bigger and much more complex picture. The same goes for our towns and cities. While they might seem like they are divided from nature, they are still part of it.

The same goes for Zion National Park. This park is not a standalone monument. Eons of natural forces shaped it. Specifically, as said before, Zion Canyon was formed by the Virgin River. The Native Americans had named the canyon Mukuntuweap or "The Straight Canyon."

But even they knew this wasn't a solitary formation. On the contrary, this park is situated at the intersection of three major geologic provinces: the Colorado Plateau, the Great Basin, and the Mojave Desert.

In Geology, this part of the North American continent is known as the Grand Staircase. Yes, this staircase is exactly what it sounds like. A Staircase of the National Parks and Zion lies in the middle.

It is a series of colorful cliffs and plateaus in the southwestern United States, consisting of several distinct steps or rock formations. These formations represent a geologic history that spans hundreds of millions of years, forming the local desert landscape.

This staircase is made up of five main steps or layers, each of which is characterized by a different type of rock and distinct topography. In other words, every step has a particular kind of rock, color, and age. It reaches from the Grand Canyon as the lowest position, then Zion National Park to Bryce Canyon National Park.

Indeed, this plethora of landscapes is why Zion is so famous. Its diverse landscape is characterized by towering cliffs, deep canyons, and intricate rock formations. A sight for sore eyes!

Not all of us are geology buffs, but learning some basics, like the age of the rocks and their formations, is necessary in understanding the national park we visit. That especially goes for Zion since its varied geology is one of the main reasons it was proclaimed a national park.

The park's oldest rocks are granite and formed through metamorphic origin, thus making the rocks range from approximately 240 million to over 2 billion years old. They can be found in the eastern section.

Still, they are not the most well-known formations here. No, the most distinctive geologic feature of Zion National Park is the towering sandstone cliffs of Zion Canyon. These cliffs are made up of Navajo Sandstone.

Some 200 million years ago, a thick layer of rock was deposited by wind and water here. The constant flow of both is what bound the rocks together and formed this dense layer. The sandstone is highly resistant to erosion and has been sculpted into various unique shapes and formations, including arches and spires.

That is not all Zion has to offer. Due to its vast area, it also protects other monuments like the Kolob Canyons. It is a series of narrow canyons formed by the erosion of Navajo Sandstone, not known to most, but they are truly breathtaking. One can also see the Checkerboard Mesa, a distinctive rock formation with a unique pattern of horizontal and vertical lines.

Zion Landscapes

Anyone who has ever visited this national park knows one thing: There is not a more beautiful landscape than that of Zion Canyon.

We already know that Zion National Park lies in southern Utah on the edge of the Colorado Plateau. So far, we have yet to mention the nearest big cities like Las Vegas, Salt Lake City, and the closest city of Springdale, together with Orderville, and Cedar City. The park lies inside the territories of Washington, Iron, and Kane counties.

The park's highest peak is 8,726 ft high, Horse Ranch Mountain, while the lowest elevation is at Coal Pits Wash at 3,666 ft. This vast area of 146,500 acres with an elevation difference of 5,000 ft has enough space to host four habitat types, all kinds of wild flora and fauna, and offers us an array of beauty.

This is the place where the Virgin River forms from scarce desert waters. These waters have been working for millennia to build the canyons and towers that stand tall today. Its constantly changing landscape offers checkerboard prints, lowland deserts, and occasional forests.

This river is a lifeline for the greenery that grows here, and it offers shelter and livelihood, not just to humans. Animals and plants also thrive due to their constant flow. That is why we can surely say that Zion National Park boasts an incredible range of landscapes. At the same time, each has its unique features and characteristics.

The park's beauty is a testament to the water's power and the rock's resilience. Truly, this is a heaven and an oasis in one. Zion is also home to diverse ecosystems, from riparian areas along the river to alpine meadows at the highest elevations.

As repeated, the streams and rivers have carved out deep, narrow canyons in the rock. Which has formed the park's most iconic features, like the Narrows and Zion Canyon. The force of water creates various terraces and floodplains, allowing life to thrive.

Overall, Zion National Park's landscapes are breathtaking. If you ask me, these are some of the most stunning natural wonders of the world. Today, around 125,000 acres of land inside the park are proclaimed wilderness.

One can revel here in stone arches formed by the winds and rock columns. You can think of the numerous streams flowing into the Virgin River and the canyon. Last, but not least come the landscapes formed by man. Some of them are archeological sites, and others are still in use today and are part of the living history in the park.

Zion National Park is home to numerous archaeological sites, which might be challenging to spot due to their remote locations, but they are all there. Sites like rock drawings and houses are among them. These sites are fragile; even the slightest disturbances can make them disappear. That is why I recommend looking at petroglyphs and other rock art from a distance if you come across it.

Other locations in the valleys also have historical value. One of them is Zion Lodge. It was built in the early 1900s and was known as Mukuntuweap Lodge. The original was a rustic lodge, later expanded to house numerous tourists. It stands even today.

Six Regions of Zion

Zion National Park is divided into six regions or areas, each with its unique features and attractions. Each section has its own story and appearance, and what makes this park so special is how easy it is to distinguish each region individually.

That is why I will have to take you through every section individually on this journey through Zion. They are essential in your exploration and hiking inside the park. These are the sections of Zion National Park:

Desert Lowland

The desert lowland is a special section of Zion National Park, located in the park's driest, hottest, and lowest region. Due to its harsh climate and limited access, it is one of the least visited sections. Only a few seasoned hikers familiar with backcountry life visit this area. Still, this is a desert and not for the faint of heart.

Despite this, it still offers visitors an incredible opportunity to experience nature. That is nature in its rawest form. This section has something for everyone, from spectacular views to unique wildlife and plants.

Visitors can explore this area on foot or by taking a guided tour from one of the park's experienced rangers. Whether you're looking for a peaceful stroll or an adventure, the desert lowland will surely provide an unforgettable experience!

Still, you will need to be prepared for desert life and backpacking. Water will be scarce, and venturing here during summer is not recommended. Therefore, if you plan to hike here, ensure you have the knowledge and skills needed.

Kolob Canyons

Kolob Canyons is a unique and isolated section of Zion National Park. It lies in the northwestern part of the park, a secluded wilderness full of majestic sandstone cliffs and lush vegetation.

Truthfully, if you want to see canyons that are more than Zion Canyon, these are your best (and less popular) ones. It features several hiking trails of varying difficulty, including the famous Taylor Creek Trail.

Kolob Canyons has a separate entrance fee from the main canyon area. This section has its own Visitor Center with exhibits, a bookstore, and a picnic area.

Kolob Terrace

This high-elevation road lies in the western part of Zion National Park. It is the highest part of the park, with an elevation range of 3,800 to 8,726 feet above sea level.

This is the place to be if you are looking for amazing views. You can take a shuttle or your own car via this road to reach the peak of the Terrace. This section offers some of the most spectacular views in Zion.

Most people drive to the top of the terrace. This drive offers breathtaking views of rock cliffs and canyons below. Here, you can visit and see the so-called Subway.

Overall, Kolob Terrace is a must-see destination for all visitors to Zion National Park, offering a stunning mix of natural beauty and outdoor adventure. Even if you are not a hiker or someone in your group is feeling down, this drive is a great option to revel in the natural beauty of Zion.

Zion Narrows

The Zion Narrows is a section of Zion National Park known for its dramatic and narrow canyon walls. The hike through the

19

Narrows is considered one of the park's most memorable and unique experiences.

The trail takes visitors through the Virgin River, which runs through the canyon and creates a unique hiking experience. It is truly a breathtaking experience!

The walls of the Zion Narrows reach up to 1,000 feet in height and provide a stunning backdrop for the hike. Visitors can see the unique geological formations and rock layers that have been carved out over millions of years.

One can customize the hike through the Narrows to fit different skill levels and preferences. Some visitors hike just a short distance into the canyon, while others roam the entire canyon. The hike requires wading and sometimes swimming through the river, so proper gear is essential.

Upper East Canyon

Now, this is a place for those that enjoy a scenic drive! If you or someone in your group doesn't feel like hiking, this is the place to enjoy it with your own vehicle. Why? Because there are numerous resting stops, places to photograph, and enjoy the view.

Upper East Canyon is a breathtaking Zion National Park section with a scenic drive along Route 9. You will see all types of rock formations and go through the iconic Zion - Mt. Carmel Tunnel.

Here, visitors can explore and take photographs at various points along the drive. One of the highlights of this section is Checkerboard Mesa, a unique rock formation with a distinctive grid-like pattern. Overall, Upper East Canyon is a must-visit for anyone who wants to experience the full natural beauty of Zion National Park.

Main Canyon

Last but not least is the main canyon, once known as Mukuntuweap or Little Zion Canyon. It is the most popular section of Zion National Park. Most of the park's iconic features and trails are located here.

It is often the busiest part of the park, and has many popular trails and landmarks, such as Angels Landing, the Great White Throne, Weeping Rock, Emerald Pools, Zion Lodge, and the Visitor Center. This is also where visitors can catch the park's free shuttle, which runs through the park and takes one to trailheads and viewpoints.

Wildlife Of Zion

The lifeline of Zion Park is its river, and due to its lush water, which gives life to the desert, numerous species of animals and plants live near it. We should respect wildlife, so avoid animals and never pick plants. This way, we can ensure that future generations can have the possibility to enjoy Zion too.

The park's wildlife includes coyotes, red foxes, and black bears mainly. The local desert landscape is home to animals like rattlesnakes, lizards, and the iconic desert bighorn sheep. You may encounter wildlife like mountain lions and bobcats (rarely) and smaller creatures like chipmunks, squirrels, and various birds.

It is a birdwatcher's paradise, with over 200 species of birds recorded here. The list includes golden eagles, peregrine falcons, and California condors. The park is home to over 1,000 species of plants as well. The most common being sagebrush, yucca, cactus, and various species of grasses.

In terms of plants, you can find desert plants such as creosote bush, mesquite, and black brush. As you climb higher in height, you will encounter juniper, pinyon pine, and ponderosa pine trees.

If you travel along the Virgin River, you are sure to see cottonwood and willow trees. Another thing I enjoy is the hanging gardens that cling to the steep canyon walls, with ferns, mosses, and wildflowers growing there.

In the park's higher elevations, you can find alpine plants such as alpine fir, engelmann spruce, and bristlecone pine. These hardy plants have adapted through the ages to the harsh mountain environment.

It's important to remember to treat these wild plants and animals with respect and lots of caution. Visitors should avoid approaching or feeding wild animals and plucking flowers or plants. Remember, it is part of the leave-no-trace policy!

What Can I Do in Zion?

Besides hiking, which is this book's main theme, you can also enjoy numerous other guided tours and self-guided adventures here. Almost no outdoor activity can't be done in Zion National Park. That is, depending on your interests and physical abilities. Here are some ideas:

- Hiking: Zion is a hiker's paradise! The trails range from easy nature walks to thru-hikers and multi-day backpacking trips.

- Scenic drives: Zion has some of the most breathtaking scenic drives in the country.

- Rock climbing: Zion's sandstone cliffs attract rock climbers from all over the world, with various routes for climbers of all skill levels.

- Biking: The Pa'rus Trail is a paved bike path that winds through Zion Canyon, perfect for those that love two wheels.

- Wildlife watching: Keep your eyes peeled while hiking or take a guided wildlife tour!

- Evening programs: Sleepover in the desert wilderness with a guide sounds terrific.

- Camping: Reservations are strongly recommended during peak season, but more on this soon.

- Water activities: Check the park's current river conditions before venturing out.

- Photography: Zion is a photographer's dream. Don't forget your camera!

- New activities like canyoneering, fishing, horseback riding, stargazing, and numerous others!

Apart from the rest of the park, the Virgin River also hosts numerous sports to try. You can enjoy swimming, tubing, and kayaking here. However, the Virgin River can also pose a danger to visitors. She can bring on flash floods, which can be sudden and deadly.

Other weather conditions, like snow and storms, are to be seen here, making it essential for visitors to stay informed about weather conditions. Therefore, be sure you have all the gear or be ready to rent some while having all the outdoor skills needed because Zion is a beautiful but unforgiving place!

Conclusion

Once we have reached the end of this section, it is time to discuss everything we have learned so far. Remember, always check the official site, or ask rangers about the situation of the trail. Be aware that flash floods can occur, and you should not touch or feed animals or pick plants.

Remember that when living with nature and showing her your respect, she will show you hers too. Therefore, prepare yourself to learn all about this wonder of the desert, and most importantly, don't forget to enjoy your adventure!

LODGING

I remember the old times when my family and I were about to start visiting national parks. Believe me, with four girls, planning and research were a nightmare. I think I've seen it all.

That is why I understand the numerous concerns you are having. This goes especially for beginners who don't really know where to start. Should they book a hotel, bed, and breakfast or jump into camping?

Well, I will tell you one thing that is for sure: Not everyone loves camping. That especially goes for those light sleepers and people who love to sleep in a bed! As I said, I've seen it all, and it's not a big deal. The only catch is for you and your group to be honest with each other.

If someone doesn't like sleeping in a tent or wants a more luxurious getaway with their partner, it's not a huge deal to share that with your team. Therefore, make sure you know what you and your family/friends/significant other have in mind regarding sleeping arrangements, and only then should you make reservations.

I also understand that many people are scared of camping, so make sure you discuss this with your group too. Last but not least, a lot of people think it is unhygienic, don't want to use the same bathroom as others, and lastly, want to shower every evening/morning/other time of day. Of course, some individuals can't camp due to medical reasons. Make sure you don't push your team, or you might end up camping alone!

Therefore, finding suitable lodging is one of the most important considerations when planning a trip to a national park (or anywhere else). This lodging or campsite can be to your liking: Near, far, silent, busy, extravagant, minimal, etc.

As said before, there are various options for lodging near nature. They can be campsites too, as well as lodges and hotels. Each park has its own location and environment, so different types of accommodation will be available all over.

In other words, you will be able to find campsites anywhere, while resorts might not always be available. Therefore, first, define what suits your needs. Some national parks have lodging options within the park itself! Others, on the other hand, require you to stay outside the park and commute. It all depends on the location.

Zion National Park, the park we are interested in, is one of the parks that offers accommodation options inside the park perimeters. You can choose to stay in campsites (like any other park) or find accommodation located inside the park. You can also choose accommodations outside the park or in nearby towns and cities.

Still, that is only part of it when it comes to lodging. Like visits to the park itself, even the lodging demand has drastically increased. Therefore, the need for lodging near national parks has risen in recent years. That is, primarily during peak seasons, so booking your accommodation well in advance is essential. Additionally, the prices for lodging near national parks can vary widely. That is mainly depending on the location and the type of accommodation.

Tips For Lodging

Before we begin with our lodging recommendations, we must get a few tips out there. They will help you understand your lodging and what to expect and prepare you for what lies ahead. With that being said, don't let these preparations scare you.

On the contrary, let them excite you to try new things. Even if you are staying in a hotel room, the fact that you are near the outdoors and living your dream should make you proud. It is a step in the right direction!

Also, it's completely understandable for people to be concerned about lodging. They are visiting national parks for the first time and don't know what to expect. Accommodations can book up quickly, especially during peak seasons, so these tips are there to prepare you for everything. Here are a few things to keep in mind:

- Think ahead and research and book your lodging as early as possible. It will ensure availability since you will be the early bird!

- Search inside the park first and then outside. Nothing is better than waking up in a national park; these mornings are the best for me! Many national parks have their own lodging options located inside the park. These options can be booked directly through their website, and everything else in the park will be near.

- If disaster strikes, act cool! If the national park's lodging is fully booked, consider alternative options. These can be nearby campgrounds, vacation rentals, or glamping options, all located near the entrance. These will also be much cheaper!

- If you want to avoid the crowd, choose your time carefully. Consider visiting the national park during the shoulder seasons. It doesn't just help you avoid groups, but more lodging options are available.

- Last but most important is the traveler's guide to happiness: Go with the flow! Sometimes, unexpected changes in your travel plans can lead to incredible adventures. Stay tuned for what each park has to offer, and if you cannot find lodging inside, consider exploring other nearby areas.

Lodging Inside Zion National Park

As someone with numerous experiences with camping and staying over in countless national parks, I love staying inside the park premises. It has many advantages, including being close to trailheads and having early access.

It minimizes crowds and allows you to see the park in all its glory. I love spending all of my time inside the park! If you try it, I am sure you will enjoy it too. Additionally, staying inside the park allows for more flexibility. After half-day hikes, you can return to your lodging, eat lunch and head back out quickly.

It's important to note that lodging inside Zion National Park can be quite expensive, so ensure you are prepared. Since only one lodge is available, you can foresee that availability can be limited.

That especially goes during peak seasons and winter when most people don't want to camp. Therefore, if you plan on staying here, booking your lodging well in advance might be a good idea. Needless to say, be prepared to pay a premium price. But it is worth it for the convenience of staying inside the park if you ask me!

These are the lodging options available inside the park:

1. Zion National Park Lodge

2. Campsites - There are three major campsites inside the park. More on them later.

Zion National Park Lodge

The Zion National Park Lodge has stood since 1919, offering visitors a chance to experience the park's natural beauty and rich history. This is all done in comfort and style. The lodge features cabins and hotel rooms, but there is more. Here you can dine in one of the two restaurants, visit the gift shop, and a free shuttle service to explore the park is also available.

This is the only in-park lodging option available! Therefore, as said above, expect high prices and numerous other guests. You will need to book much longer in advance. Therefore, to make sure you are getting what you need for your buck, make sure you know everything about this lodging option.

The Lodge lies in the heart of Zion Canyon, where the first European settlers built their homes. It allows guests to be in close proximity to the park's main attractions. In other words, you can be anywhere in only a few minutes, including the Emerald Pools, Weeping Rock, and the Zion Narrows. The Zion Canyon Visitor Center, where visitors can get information about park activities and guided tours, is also close by.

For me, Zion Lodge is the epitome of Zion National Park. One of the benefits of staying at Zion Lodge is the early access, which I love since I am a morning person. I take advantage of the quiet mornings to hike and explore the park since there is something new every season.

If you are visiting during hotter months, I recommend you return to the lodge for a break during the heat of the day. That is another pro for this accommodation option!

You won't stay hungry since Zion Lodge also offers on-site dining options. You can find a seat in one of the restaurants or use the snack bar. There's also a gift shop where visitors can purchase souvenirs and supplies. In terms of the accommodation itself, one can choose between the hotel, suite, and cabins.

Most people stay in the hotel, where the rooms have two beds, while some are single and offer a king-size bed. All of them have a porch or balcony and are exceptionally clean. If you choose to stay in the suite, you will also have a sitting room that offers more space to visitors.

Of course, cabins are also popular, with 40 cabins altogether. Some are two-bed, and some are single queen-bed cabins, while all have a fireplace, porch, kitchen, and bath. In terms of luxury, these are simple options.

The whole Lodge offers free Wi-Fi, air conditioning, free parking, irons and boards, hair dryers, and coffee machines, just like your everyday hotel. In the end, this is nothing fancy but perfect for nature lovers who don't or can't camp but want to stay in the center of the park.

Zion National Park Lodge information in short:

- Offering: hotel and suite rooms and cabins, one and two bedrooms
- Minimal stay: None
- Reservation: Yes, can be canceled for free
- Pets: No
- Wi-Fi: Yes
- Food on site: Yes
- Free parking: Yes
- Wheelchair accessible: Yes
- Kitchen: Yes
- Toilet: Yes

Pros:

- In the center of the park
- Clean
- Simple
- Free Wi-Fi and parking

Cons:

- Busy
- Often booked out
- Expensive
- No pets

Campsites In Zion National Park

Do you want to feel free and live with nature, even if it might be just for a short weekend? Then, camping is perfect for you. Take your RV if you want, or it doesn't have to be anything fancy; you and your tent can seal the deal.

In addition to camping being a fun experience, doing it in Zion Canyon is an unforgettable ordeal. It is a great way to immerse yourself in the park's natural beauty and enjoy the great desert.

Zion National Park has several camping regulations to ensure a safe and enjoyable camping experience for all visitors. So, if you plan on camping inside the park, make sure to understand them. They include:

- A maximum stay of 14 nights
- Restrictions on open fires and collecting firewood
- Up to 6 people per campsite
- Two vehicles or one RV per campsite
- Food stored in a container or car
- Two tents per campsite
- Leashed pets allowed

Like most parks and maintained campsites, visitors can still have access to several amenities. If you are reaching the park without a car, worry not. The park offers a shuttle service that stops at each campground. Restrooms with flushable toilets and running water are available at almost every campground.

As mentioned, camping can be quite popular, and campsites can fill up quickly, especially during peak seasons here. It's a good idea to make early reservations so you know when and where you will be camping for your vacation. Remember that before leaving, you will also have to check the park's website for any updates or alerts.

Campgrounds available inside Zion National Park include:

1. Watchman Campground

2. South Campground

3. Lava Point Campground

Watchman Campground

Lying just below the Watchman, this campsite is one of my (and others) favorites. Just a short walk from the park's Visitor Center and along the Virgin River, it is an excellent location for hikers and campers alike. One can easily access the river for fishing and swimming, but the whole park is also at your disposal in a few steps.

The campground is open year-round. It offers 200 campsites, including tent and RV sites. Each site has a picnic table and fire pit, and restrooms with flush toilets and running water are located throughout the campground. One can make reservations for Watchman Campground up to six months in advance. Believe me, these are a must.

If you are traveling with an RV, there is a dump station, as well as potable water. You will also find a camp store that sells everything you might need: firewood, ice, and other camping essentials.

Here are the basics for this site:

- Offering: 200 campsites

- Minimal stay: None

- Reservation: Yes, can be canceled
- Dogs: Yes
- Wi-Fi: Yes
- Food on site: Yes
- Free parking: Yes
- Toilet: Yes

Pros:

- In the center of the park
- Up to 2 vehicles per site
- Clean

Cons:

- Busy
- Often booked out

South Campground

This campground is smaller and less popular but perfect for bigger groups. I tend to camp here not only when the Watchman Campground is booked out but also because it lies in a wooded area. It is perfect for the summer months when the temperatures are high since the site provides plenty of shade and privacy.

It offers 117 campsites, including tent and RV sites. Restrooms have flushable toilets and running water. The campground is open from early March to the end of October, and reservations can be made up to 14 days early.

The regulations like a maximum stay of 14 nights, a limit of six people per site, and fire restrictions are also in place here. Overall, South Campground is an excellent option for visitors who want to experience Zion National Park through a more rustic and secluded setting.

This is what you need to know about this site:

- Offering: 117 campsites

- Minimal stay: None

- Reservation: Yes, can be canceled

- Dogs: Yes

- Wi-Fi: Yes

- Food on site: Yes

- Free parking: Yes

- Toilet: Yes

Pros:

- Secluded

- Private

Cons:

- Smaller

- Often booked out

Lava Point Campground

About 1 hour and 20 minutes from the south entrance and at an elevation of 7,900 feet lies Lava Point Campground. It is a scenic campground site with stunning views of the surrounding canyons and mountains, perfect for wildlife watching and stargazing.

The campground is typically open from May through September if the weather allows. It offers six primitive campsites with picnic tables and fire rings. Restrooms consist of pit toilets. Amenities such as potable water, showers, or electrical hookups are unavailable here. One key piece of advice: bring your own water and other supplies and pack out all trash.

Lodging In Springdale

I understand if you don't want to spend a whole fortune on a national park and hiking vacation. On the contrary, lodging should be the least expensive part of your trip. Still, we are here to enjoy nature, not a rented room.

That is why most people choose to find their accommodation options elsewhere. The closest town near Zion National Park is Springdale, Utah. The lower rates and accessibility make it a great time and money saver.

Springdale is located in Washington County, Utah, at an elevation of 3,900 feet and right below Zion National Park. It is a small desert town that comes to life during the peak season or summer. Stunning red rock cliffs and canyons surround this small town. It is civilization.

During the peak tourism season, the town's population can swell to several thousand. That is due to the influx of visitors to the national park. Many visitors choose to stay in the city due to its proximity to the park. In addition to Zion National Park, Springdale has several galleries, shops, and restaurants catering to tourists.

In terms of lodging, there are several options. It includes hotels, motels, and vacation rentals. Many of these properties lie within walking distance of the park's entrance. Since you will be near the park, the primary mode of transportation in Springdale is by car or shuttle. The shuttle stops at several points in Springdale and Zion.

Overall, Springdale is a charming small town. Throughout its history, it served as the gateway to Zion National Park. The city provides visitors with a range of lodging and dining options, and here are some of them:

Airbnb

This is your deal if you are looking for luxury just outside the entrance! Plenty of Airbnb homes are available just minutes away from the park's entrance. This particular Nama-Stay Airbnb vacation home offers wide-open views designed to be in harmony with nature. The best part? It is located in downtown Springdale. Five minutes away from the park's South entrance, grocery stores, restaurants, and various outdoor activities.

This Zen-like home is perfect for small retreats or families and hosts up to eight people. It offers three bedrooms, 2.5 bathrooms, a full kitchen, and a back patio, perfect for you! The views are spectacular!

This is the most important information in short:

- Offering: 3 bedrooms

- Minimal stay: None

- Reservation: Yes

- Pets: No

- Wi-Fi: Yes

- Food on site: No

- Free parking: Yes

- Wheelchair accessible: Unknown

- Kitchen: Yes

- Toilet: Yes

Pros:

- Near the entrance

- Amazing views

- Free Wi-Fi and parking

Cons:

- Often booked out

- Expensive

- No pets

Zion Canyon Lodge

This amazing hotel gem is just 3 minutes from the South entrance to Zion National Park. If you are looking for a budget-friendly location that can host anyone and cater to their needs, then this is your best bet.

Choose between a family suite or a standard room; you will get a kitchenette and a full bathroom. Most visitors think this is one of the best budget-friendly options here. You can check it out and see if you agree.

Here is what you need to know:

- Offering: Family suite or standard room

- Minimal stay: None

- Reservation: Yes, can be canceled

- Pets: No

- Wi-Fi: Yes

- Food on site: No

- Free parking: Yes

- Wheelchair accessible: Yes

- Kitchen: Yes

- Toilet: Yes

Pros:

- Near the entrance

- Budget-friendly

- Free Wi-Fi and parking

Cons:

- No pets

Watchman Villas

If you are looking for a place to stay far away from the season's hustle and bustle while not being afraid of spending a bit more, the Watchman Villas is your best option. 1 mile from the entrance in a newly constructed village near the park is this beauty. Each villa hosts up to 8 people, and depending on the type of apartment you get, they have a balcony, full kitchen, and sitting area.

Basic information in short:

- Offering: 5 villas with 1 or 2 bedrooms
- Minimal stay: None
- Reservation: Yes, can be canceled
- Pets: Yes
- Wi-Fi: Yes
- Food on site: No
- Free parking: Yes
- Wheelchair accessible: No
- Kitchen: Yes
- Toilet: Yes

Pros:

- Secluded
- Pet friendly
- Free Wi-Fi and parking

Cons:

- Expensive
- 1 mi from the entrance

Zion Wildflower Glamping

Do you want to try elevated camping or tiny home lodging? Well, Zion Wildflower Resort is a great place to start! One can choose from luxury tents or private bungalows and camp in style! In fact, to match the desert theme, this glamping site also made its own covered wagons, in which you can sleep.

This is what you need to know:

- Offering: Bungalows, wagon, tent glamping options
- Minimal stay: None
- Reservation: Yes, can be canceled
- Pets: No
- Wi-Fi: Yes
- Food on site: No
- Free parking: Yes
- Wheelchair accessible: No
- Kitchen: No
- Toilet: Yes

Pros:

- Reasonably priced
- Wagons
- Free Wi-Fi and parking
- Near entrance

Cons:

- Wi-Fi doesn't work often

Other Lodging

Not everyone enters Zion through the south entrance or Springdale. No, some people also reach it via the north entrance. There are several towns near Zion National Park. They all offer additional lodging options.

Hurricane, 25 miles from Zion National Park, is a great place to stay. It has excellent views and is bigger than Springdale. It offers a range of budget-friendly lodging options, including hotels and motels. The town also has several restaurants and shops.

Cedar City is the biggest city near Zion. It is also the furthest away, about 60 miles from the park. But apart from Zion, it hosts several cultural attractions, so you won't be bored there either.

With that being said, you do know that some of these towns require a longer drive. As mentioned above, you will need more gas to get to Zion National Park. Still, they offer more affordable lodging options and additional amenities that are not available within the park or in Springdale.

Conclusion

In the end, remember to go with the flow when it comes to lodging and expect everything, even in terms of weather. Plan in advance, since in the peak season; everything could be booked.

Make sure your whole group is ready and comfortable with your lodging choice, and then off goes the reservation.

Ultimately, the decision on where to stay depends on you. If you prioritize being as close as possible to Zion's trails and don't mind a more rustic experience and expensive rate, staying inside the park may be the best option. However, staying in Springdale may be a better choice if you value more amenities and want to be close to other attractions outside the park. Decide yourself!

ENTRANCE FEES & PERMITS

Most people think that entrance fees and staying inside national parks are skyrocketing prices. You would not believe that most parks have free entrance. Still, we also need to remember that these fees are there to protect our nature for future generations too!

Therefore, before entering any park, you will need to know that entrance fees for national parks in the US are charged to help support the maintenance and upkeep of the parks. The fees are used to pay for various things, not just for administration or the government. By paying a fee, you also pay to keep up the local trail maintenance, visitor center operations, bathroom facilities, and other amenities that help make the parks more enjoyable.

We will discuss the fees mentioned above; more are not solely responsible for funding parks. The National Park Service also receives funding from the federal government and private donations to support its operations.

Numerous other parks and Zion National Park participate in the Federal Recreation Lands Enhancement Act. This act allows national parks to collect visitor fees and retain 80% of the funds for park maintenance, repairs, and improvements. That means when you pay $10 to the park upon entering, only $8 will go to the park.

The remaining 20% of the fees collected are deposited in a particular account. This account aims to support other parks and recreational areas where fees are not collected. This system ensures that all national parks receive funding for necessary projects and upkeep. This goes regardless of whether or not they collect entrance fees. In other words, from the $10 you paid, $2 goes to other parks.

I know I have said it numerous times, but I need to underline that Zion National Park is one of the most visited national parks in the United States. To ensure the park's preservation and upkeep, all visitors must purchase a recreational use pass before entering. In other words, entering the park is free, but recreationally using the premises is paid.

You don't have to buy only one pass every time you enter through those gates. The park offers a variety of pass options to meet the needs of different visitors. These passes include weekly, annual, lifetime, and many other options.

The weekly pass is ideal for those who plan to visit the park for a short period, stay inside or near the park, and plan to visit it every day of their stay. The annual pass is perfect for frequent visitors that live near the area. And a lifetime pass is an excellent option for those who want to support the park's preservation and plan to visit multiple national parks throughout their lifetime.

It is important to note that the entrance fee for Zion National Park is not just a fee to access the park. National parks are important for their ecological, historical, and cultural significance. The revenue generated from the passes helps support the park's maintenance and operations.

That is why ensuring they are properly maintained and protected is essential, so our kids and grandkids can enjoy them too! Therefore, you must remember that you support the natural environment while paying a fee.

Overall, purchasing a recreational use pass for Zion National Park is an excellent way to support the park's preservation efforts while enjoying the natural beauty and recreational opportunities.

Entrance Fee Prices

Now let's get to it. What are the entrance fee prices? How can you get them? Are they cheap or pricey? Don't worry. They are not that pricey. On the contrary, you will see that the entrance fee is relatively inexpensive here.

Remember, these passes are crucial for supporting the park's maintenance and operations. If you want to be part of helping to preserve the park's natural resources for future generations to enjoy, a pass is the best way to do so.

Weekly Passes

Weekly Passes are an excellent option for those who plan to visit the park for a shorter period. It is valid for seven days from the date of purchase. A few options available for weekly passes are:

- A private vehicle pass costs $35 and admits a non-commercial vehicle (15-passenger capacity or less) and all occupants to the park's Zion Canyon and Kolob Canyon areas.

- A per-person pass costs $20 and admits one individual without a car to the park, typically used for bicyclists, hikers, and pedestrians. The best part? Youth aged 15 and under are admitted free.

- A motorcycle pass costs $30 and admits one non-commercial motorcycle to the park.

Annual Passes

Annual Passes are a cost-effective option for frequent visitors. It is valid for one year from the date of purchase. A few options available are:

- The Zion Annual Pass costs $70

- Military Annual Passes are Free.

- Senior Annual Passes are $20. It is available to all citizens and residents over the age of 62 years. Documentation of age and residency or citizenship is required. This pass gives you access to all Federal fee areas for one year.

We need to set some boundaries here since you need to be educated in terms of fees, especially if you are a first-time visitor. All visitors entering the park, even those passing through, must purchase a park pass.

I love that Zion National Park only sells park passes in person, and you can buy them at any entrance station. You can purchase your pass using cash, a debit card, or a credit card.

Remember the crucial parts: These passes are non-transferable and can be purchased using a credit card. Needless to say, seniors, military officials, volunteers, and veterans all receive a discount. Here is an easy way of sorting out these prices:

Type of Passes	Price
Day pass	Not offered
Teenagers and kids below 15 years of age	Free
Weekly pass per person	$20
Weekly pass per car	$35
Weekly pass per motorcycle	$30
Annual Zion pass	$70
Military Annual pass	Free
Senior Annual pass	$20

Permits

You might not believe it, but permits are not just there to collect money. Permits are there to protect nature. Apart from being required to enter certain areas of national parks in the US, these permits are intended to protect the safety of visitors, preserve the park's natural resources, and manage the impact of human activities on the park's ecosystems.

In some cases, permits are required for popular activities that may pose safety risks. They are often required for backcountry camping and hiking in remote park areas. This way, park officials can ensure that visitors are adequately prepared and equipped.

Most people don't understand the logic behind permits. The main goal is that they can limit the number of visitors in a given area to prevent overcrowding. The National Parks Administration has learned that this is the best way to manage the impact of human activities on ecosystems.

Of course, not all park activities need permits, or else no one would visit them anymore.

Permits are separate from the park entrance fee; only some need to pay depending on their activity. For example, permits for activities like canyoneering, rock climbing, or off-road vehicle use may be required. All of these activities can cause damage to fragile landscapes and wildlife habitats.

If you plan to hike in certain areas of the park, such as Angels Landing, or camp in a designated campground, you will also need a permit. For canyoneering or other backcountry activities, permits are required to help protect fragile wilderness areas and ensure visitor safety. These permits can be obtained through the park's website or at the Visitor Center.

It is important to note that permit fees vary depending on the activity and location and are non-refundable. Additionally, obtaining a permit only guarantees access to a specific location if it hasn't reached its capacity limit.

Wilderness Permit

As you might know, Zion is full of wilderness. And the park does not keep its visitors from enjoying it. When doing certain activities to ensure the preservation of these areas, the park requires Wilderness permits and charges a fee based on the group size.

If you need clarification on the goal of this fee, worry not. A lot of people can't wrap their heads around it. This fee is only paid by people that enter or sleep in the wilderness or backcountry areas of the park.

The Wilderness fee includes only certain activities like hiking the more strenuous trails such as the Narrows Top-Down, entering or sleeping over in the wild, and similar activities happening outback.

Remember, not everyone needs to pay the Wilderness fee! If you plan on engaging in these activities, there is a $5 non-refundable reservation fee plus as follows: $15 for 1 to 2 people, $20 for 3 to 7 people, and $25 for 8 to 12 people.

These fees help fund critical projects such as trail maintenance, wildlife protection, and visitor education in wilderness areas. It is important to note that Wilderness permits are non-transferable and must be obtained before your visit. Here is a visualization again:

Wilderness fees	Price
1-2 people	$15
3-7 people	$20
8-12 people	$25

In summary, the park entrance fee is required for everyone, while permits are required to enter certain areas and not for everyone. They do not just protect the safety of visitors, as most of us might think. The main goal is to preserve the park's natural resources. We all want them to be there so that the next generations can enjoy them too.

How To Acquire a Permit?

As stated above, you may need a permit if you want to hike in certain areas of Zion National Park. There are two ways to get a permit: the Seasonal Lottery and the Day-Before Lottery.

Still, you need to know things before applying for a permit. Check the Zion National Park website to see if the activity you plan to do requires a permit. Often people apply for permits that don't even exist.

Once you determine that you need a permit, you can apply for it through the Zion National Park website or recreation.gov. The website will provide specific instructions on how to apply for the type of permit you need. As said before, a fee is typically associated with permits in Zion National Park. You can pay the fee online at the time of application.

The processing time for permits can vary, so make sure to allow enough time for your permit to be approved before your planned activity. For instance, if you plan to hike in June, July, or August, you would apply for the Seasonal Lottery in April.

Below are the activities that require a permit. Later we will address some of these permits.

- Backcountry backpacking
- Angels Landing

- Narrows

- Subway

- Virgin River

- Rock Climbing

- Canyoneering

- Stock use

Seasonal Lottery

You will choose seven days and time windows of days and times you want to hike. You must pay a non-refundable fee of $6 per application to apply, covering up to 6 people. If you get approved, you will be charged $3 per person.

You will receive an email notification about your application status, and if approved, you must print your permit since mobile phone service is unreliable at the checkpoint. You should know that permit applications are taken well in advance. For instance, you apply in January to hike in March to May, in April for June to August, in July for September to November, and finally in October for December through February.

Day-Before Lottery

If you didn't get to apply for a seasonal permit, this is your last chance! You can apply the day before your hike, but that does not guarantee you will get a permit.

For the Day-Before Lottery, you can apply between 12:01 AM and 3 PM MT the day before your hike. The permit will be issued at 4 PM MT on the same day you apply. You will be charged the same fee as the Seasonal Lottery when approved.

Cancellations

If you need to cancel your Seasonal Lottery permit, you can do so two days before the permit RSVP date. This goes for a full $3 refund per person, but the $6 application fee is non-refundable.

If you cancel, your Seasonal Lottery will automatically roll into the Day-Before Lottery. For the Day-Before Lottery, cancellation is not allowed, and fees are non-refundable.

You can change the number of people in your group for the Seasonal Lottery, but you cannot increase the number, change the date, transfer the permit, or change to an alternate leader. You will receive a $3 refund per person if you decrease the number of applicants. This must be done two days before the RSVP date. However, for the Day-Before Lottery, permit changes are not allowed.

Permit For Angels Landing

Here comes one of my favorite hikes, which has required a permit starting April 2022. Angels Landing is one of the most popular and dangerous hikes in Zion National Park, attracting visitors from around the world.

However, due to the hike's steep drop-offs and narrow exposed trail, a permit is required to hike beyond the Scouts' Lookout to the summit. You can get your permit by logging in to your account on recreation.gov.

You can apply for a permit before your trip through the seasonal lottery. This means you'll get to pick seven ranked days and times or windows of days and times you want to hike. Keep in mind that it costs $6 to apply for a seasonal permit, which covers an application for up to 6 people (including the person filling out the application).

When they issue permits, recreation.gov will send you an email notifying you if you got a permit and have been charged $3 for each person you registered. If you cancel your permit at least two days before your hike, we will refund the $3 per person fee.

If you are late, you can apply for a permit the day before your planned hike. The lottery opens daily at 12:01 AM and closes at 3 PM. Mountain Time (MT). For example, if you plan to hike on a Tuesday, you should apply on Monday. The permits will be issued at 4 PM MT on Monday.

The permit is valid for one day only and can be used by the whole group. It's important to note that the permit does not guarantee you a spot on the trail, as there is a capacity limit to prevent overcrowding.

The permit requirement for Angels Landing is in place to ensure the safety of hikers and to help preserve the natural environment. The trail can be dangerous for inexperienced or unprepared hikers, and overcrowding can lead to accidents and damage the fragile ecosystem.

If you plan to hike Angels Landing, it's important to come prepared with proper hiking gear and to be aware of the trail's challenges. The trail is steep and strenuous, with sheer drop-offs and narrow sections that require holding onto chains for support. It's also important to stay on the designated trail to avoid damaging the delicate ecosystem.

Permit For Narrows Top-Down

The Narrows has multiple hiking options, but if you plan to hike the entire 16-mile Virgin River Narrows Top-Down trail from Chamberlain's Ranch to the Temple of Sinawava in Zion National Park, you'll need a Wilderness Permit.

This option requires arranging your own transportation to the Chamberlain's Ranch trailhead. The hike takes around 10 to 14 hours and involves an elevation change of 1,300 ft. You can split it into two days by obtaining an overnight backpacking permit.

Please note that pets are not allowed on this trail. Wilderness permits are always required for this certain hike, and you can visit the Virgin River Narrows Permits page for more detailed information. A permit is essential for preserving the park's natural beauty and ensuring a safe and enjoyable hiking experience.

This permit falls under the "Canyoneering Day Trips" category, and you can find it on the Zion Wilderness Reservations Login page. To RSVP, use the Calendar RSVP feature. There is a non-refundable fee of $5 for the RSVP.

If the RSVP is full, you can still enter the Last-Minute Drawing lottery. You can submit your application for the drawing seven days before your planned trip until noon, only two days before. The drawing is held two days before the trip, and you will be notified via email if you are selected.

Permit For Subway

To hike the Left Fork (Subway) route in Zion National Park, you will also need a Wilderness Permit; there are two options: the

Bottom-Up Hiking Route and the Top-Down Canyoneering Route.

The Bottom-Up Hiking Route is a strenuous 9-mile round-trip hike through the Left Fork of North Creek that involves route finding, hiking in ankle to knee-deep water, and scrambling over large boulders. This route begins and ends at the Left Fork Trailhead on the Kolob Terrace Road.

The Top-Down Canyoneering Route is a very strenuous 9.5-mile through-hike that requires rappelling skills, 60 feet of rope, and extensive route-finding experience. The route starts at the Wildcat Canyon Trailhead and ends at the Left Fork Trailhead, located on the Kolob Terrace Road.

Permits are required for both routes and can be obtained through the Zion National Park website. For the Bottom-Up Hiking Route, a permit is needed and can be obtained through the online reservation system at recreation.gov or by entering a lottery system.

For the Top-Down Canyoneering Route, it can only be obtained through a lottery system. It is important to carefully plan and prepare for either of these challenging hikes, as they require significant physical exertion and technical skill.

To apply for a permit, choose the Advance lottery (2 months ahead), Calendar lottery (1 month ahead), or last-minute draws (2 to 7 days in advance). You will also need to pay a non-refundable fee of $5 per calendar or last-minute lottery reservation.

If applying for the top-down hike, you must also provide proof of technical canyoneering skills and equipment. If approved, print out a copy of your permit and bring it with you on the hike.

Still, it takes work. Note that permits for the Subway are in high demand, and a limited number are available each day. It is recommended that you apply for a permit several months in advance to increase your chances of obtaining one.

Reservations

So far, we have talked about accommodation options in Zion National Park, but I think it's not a bad idea to remind you of reservations. You can make reservations for camping and some activities through Recreation.gov or by calling 877-444-6777.

Watchman Campground is open year-round, and one can make reservations up to six months in advance. South Campground is open from early March to the end of October, and reservations can be made up to 14 days before your visit. One can also make reservations for Zion Lodge this way too.

Conclusion

We are reaching the end of the story about entrance and permit fees. What are the takeaways? Paying these fees not only helps to maintain the park's infrastructure and preserve its natural beauty but also ensures the safety of visitors.

This is all to manage the number of people in specific areas and minimize the impact on the environment. Acquiring permits through the proper channels and understanding their cancellation and change policies is essential. Therefore, educate yourself and be ready to pay.

TRANSPORTATION

While starting out with camping and hiking, I always thought that reaching my destination was my main goal. Little did I know how much work there is to plan out your transportation once there. This goes especially if you are going with a bigger group or your family.

You do need to know that transportation can be tricky. Therefore, planning in advance and knowing your routes or parks is the key to a great time.

It's all great until you reach the park entrance. Only then do you see how these areas have been catered to cars. I genuinely believe in walkable national parks, as they should be. Still, this is not always possible, especially when it comes to canyons.

Therefore, each park has its own story and its own way of transportation. Many National Parks operate shuttle buses that transport visitors to various locations within the park. Zion is one of these parks. It is a great way to reduce traffic congestion and pollution while allowing visitors to enjoy the scenery without worrying about driving.

With that being said, we do need to know that, as stated above, most National Parks allow visitors to bring their own vehicles into the park. However, it's important to note that some parks have limited parking and may restrict access during peak season or high-traffic periods.

Is there a better way to reach your park and move around through it? Many National Parks have bike paths and trails that allow visitors to explore the park on two wheels. Why do I love this option? Because biking is a great way to reduce your carbon footprint and get some exercise at the same time.

Still, my favorite way, and probably yours soon, too, is walking. This is a great option for those who prefer to explore the park on foot. National Parks typically have various hiking trails ranging from easy to strenuous. Many of them offer stunning views and easy ways to get around.

It's important to remember that National Parks are protected areas. Therefore, visitors should take care to follow park rules and regulations to minimize their impact on the environment. That includes staying on designated trails, respecting wildlife, and minimizing noise pollution.

Using a Private Vehicle

I know you might be coming in with a car, but always remember that they can significantly impact the environment. This includes air and noise pollution, wildlife disturbance, and damage to park infrastructure.

If you're driving or renting a vehicle, choose from an electric or hybrid one. They produce less air pollution and are better than traditional cars, plus they are a gas saver! Some National Parks offer guided horseback tours or allow visitors to explore their premises with animals.

Now, let's see what Zion has to say about it. Sure, you can go there in your vehicle. But when? How? Worry not. I have all the answers you might need.

When visiting Zion National Park, there are a few options for where to go with your car. If it is during the shuttle season (usually from late March to early November), everything is different since this is the high season. Though there is parking inside, all visitors are encouraged to park their cars in Springdale and take the free shuttle into the park to reduce traffic congestion and parking issues. But if you must, plan to arrive earlier to secure a parking spot, as it fills up quickly.

During the non-shuttle season or low season, visitors can drive on Zion Canyon Scenic Drive, but parking is limited, and the road closes once all legal parking spaces are full. Suppose you bring your car into the park; ensure you only park in designated stalls. Remember that there are also other areas of the park to explore, such as Kolob Canyons, the Kolob Terrace Road, and the park's east side, which can be accessed by car.

While cars may be a convenient way to explore National Parks, other transportation options can be more environmentally friendly. These options provide a more immersive experience in nature. In fact, the administration sees this, and certain parks have implemented restrictions on private vehicle use.

As an alternative, visitors can use shuttle systems to reduce the number of vehicles on park roads. These can be buses or trains that can provide a convenient and eco-friendly way to access the park.

But why is this so important? It's important to consider the impact of our transportation choices on the environment when visiting National Parks. Using more sustainable transportation options can help protect these beautiful and fragile natural areas for future generations.

From what I have written before, Zion National Park is heaven, but you will need transportation while inside. In other words, it is a vast space, and you will need a way to get from point A to point B, be it a shuttle, car, bike, or animal.

In fact, there is even a type of car tourism currently inside this park since the Mt. Carmel Tunnel is open to visitors. It is a scenic outlook that you need to see. Therefore, I fully recommend using your car to get there. In other terms and while hiking, I recommend using your car only sometimes.

As said above, the Zion Canyon Scenic Drive is a must-see attraction in the park. Driving your car allows you to stop and explore magnificent places along the way. As far as I am against cars, I am still for this option! However, keep in mind that the road can be narrow and winding, and RVs and trailers are often not allowed on the scenic drive.

You will need to be cautious! Whatever signs you see, heed the warnings. Also, be mindful of your vehicle's impact on the environment. Stay on designated roads and avoid disturbing wildlife. This especially goes for off-road vehicle owners!

Overall, driving your own car can be a convenient and enjoyable way to explore Zion National Park. I actually enjoyed doing so myself too! Still, it's important to plan ahead. Consider taking the park shuttle to reduce congestion and minimize your environmental impact.

Ultimately, it is up to you if you take your car inside park perimeters or not, but make sure you know all the facts before deciding!

Parking

I know what you are expecting it to be. Imagine parking lots packed full. Yes, that is exactly what it looks like on weekends and holidays. Parking in Zion National Park is limited, and it's important to park legally and responsibly to avoid citations and towed vehicles.

Myself, the rangers, and the park administration all recommend you park only in designated stalls and avoid parking along roadways or on vegetation. If the parking lot is full, don't wait for spots to open. Instead, try another lot. You can also consider parking in Springdale and using the town shuttle to reach the park.

Keep in mind that there is a charge for parking in Springdale! This especially goes during busy times, such as weekends and holidays. The park can get very crowded during this time. In the end, remember that a National Park is still a protected area.

Traffic

The same goes for traffic; I don't mean just cars. It can get crowded here in Zion National Park, especially during summer and weekends. During the non-shuttle season, the park can still get very busy when drivers are allowed on Zion Canyon Scenic Drive.

Of course, when the road closes, all legal parking spaces are full. This helps reduce illegal parking that can harm the plants and animals in the area and avoid the gridlock that could slow down emergency responders. The road typically closes in December, January, and February.

On the other hand, there is the other part of the year, which is much more crowded. From February through November, Zion can be a popular destination with long lines at the park entrance stations and limited parking that fills up quickly.

If you want to avoid delays, park in Springdale, and ride the free shuttle to the park. Luckily, this national park is enormous, and if Zion Canyon is too busy, there are other destinations to explore. Choose between Kolob Canyons, the Kolob Terrace Road, and the east side of the park.

However, if you visit during summer, expect to see many people on trails and on the park shuttle. We must all deal with it; it is crowded during the high season. Popular hikes like the Emerald Pools Trail and The Narrows can see hundreds of visitors each day!

To avoid the crowds, consider visiting in December or January or exploring less crowded areas of the park. Sadly, long lines at the entrance are unavoidable. That is unless you arrive early or late. While inside, riding a bicycle can also be a great way to explore the park.

Zion Canyon Scenic Road

This is my recommendation if you visit the park with your car or want to take a shuttle up this road. If you ask me, it is one of the most beautiful roads with breathtaking views. It is a 6-mile long drive that winds its way through the heart of Zion National Park.

Most believe this is one of the most scenic drives in the United States. It offers stunning views of towering sandstone cliffs, winding streams, and deep canyons. The road follows the Virgin River, which runs through the canyon. You can see landmarks such as The Watchman, The Great White Throne, and Angels Landing.

The road is only open to private vehicles during the non-shuttle season, typically from December through February. Or only Zion Lodge and Canyon Trail Rides guests with reservations can access this trail when the shuttles are operating.

There are several pull outs along the way that you can enjoy. There are even overlooks to take in the magnificent views of the canyon. You can picnic here or take a few pictures! The most popular overlooks include Canyon Junction, Court of the Patriarchs, and others.

Before starting, you need to know that the road can be narrow in places. You will come across a few one-lane tunnels and winding. In some of these, vehicles must alternate and drive through one at a time. Additionally, cars over a certain height or width may not be able to pass through the tunnel, and others need a permit to do so.

Kolob Terrace Road

Here comes another beautiful road you can go and explore. Visitors to Zion National Park can experience the park's unique geography and natural features by driving along the park's western side on Kolob Terrace Road. I love this section of the park because it is unexplored and away from the hustle of the canyon. The road is quite long. It covers about 25 miles, starting from Kanaraville and ending at Kolob Reservoir.

It is truly a hidden gem, with winding switchbacks and ever-so-stunning views of the valleys below. One can find numerous pull outs along the way to explore nearby trails and enjoy the scenery.

The overlook at the end of Kolob Terrace Road is one of the road's most striking features. I love spending slow afternoons here, especially if my family and I have just arrived inside the park.

This viewpoint offers sweeping views of the park below and the surrounding mountains. Although the road is open all year, it may be closed in winter due to snow and ice. Before planning a trip, visitors should consult the park's website for current road conditions.

Zion - Mt. Carmel Tunnel

Last but definitely not least comes my favorite scenic road you can take whenever you'd want to relax and enjoy the view! This Zion-Mt. Carmel Tunnel is truly a scenic drive.

It offers stunning views of the surrounding landscape. In addition to all that scenery, it is a 1.1-mile-long tunnel. A long time ago, it was carved into the park's sandstone cliffs. This was back in the 1920s.

But why would one do so? The goal of the local government was to connect the east and west sections of Zion National Park. The east part initially didn't have that many visitors, but this tunnel changed the visitor numbers and made it more widespread.

I also love this tunnel due to its long history. It is truly an engineering marvel that took three years to complete. These small wonders are what makes the tunnel so unique, leaving you to see that people once wanted you to see what they saw.

I am thinking of the windows carved into the walls that provide a glimpse of the outside world. As you drive through the tunnel, you'll see breathtaking park views, including the Great

Arch of Zion, Checkerboard Mesa, and other geological formations. You might not know this, but this tunnel is also a historic landmark due to its age!

Motorbike In Zion National Park

Another great way to experience this incredible feat of nature is motorbiking. Motorbikes are allowed inside Zion National Park, and a fee is paid at the entrance.

As a fellow road biker, I recommend motorbikes because they can be a great way to explore the park's scenic roads. Nothing is more fulfilling to me than the wind in my hair and the road in front of me, especially if the surrounding visage is as breathtaking as Zion's.

While surrounded by all of this beauty, it might be hard to think about anything else. Still, you will need to keep in mind that motorbikes are vehicles. Like any other day, you will need to wear appropriate safety gear!

Before heading out, ensure your bike is in good condition and equipped with all required safety equipment! Keep the speed limits and road rules in mind and know that the roads are narrow and winding.

Overall, riding a motorbike can be an exciting and rewarding way to experience Zion National Park. You must still take safety seriously and respect the park's rules and regulations.

Shuttle To Zion National Park

Last but not least is the free-of-charge and extra helpful shuttles that take you from the park's entrance to the trailheads. Or, if you're staying in Springdale, to the park's entrance. It is the most common way of transportation!

Zion National Park attracts a large number of visitors each year. By taking the shuttle, you can avoid the hassle of finding parking.

What I love most is that the shuttle service is a more sustainable and eco-friendly option. This service is also meant for hikers since it provides easy access to the park's popular trailheads. It drops you off directly at the trailhead, so you can immediately start your hike.

We are all used to clammy buses, but this ride is excellent! In fact, it is also an air-conditioned ride, which is especially important during the hot summer months. You can sit back, relax, and enjoy the scenic views without worrying about traffic or parking. If you haven't done all the research before leaving home, the bus will also tell you about the park's history.

One can get a free shuttle service with two routes: the Zion Canyon Shuttle Line and the Springdale Shuttle Line. Both routes operate from March to November and provide transportation to various locations within the park and town.

With so many visitors, no reservations are needed. Shuttle schedule may change every year so visitors should check the schedule beforehand. If you want to stay out of the traffic, be eco-friendly, or are on foot, the shuttle provides a convenient way to explore Zion Canyon.

The Zion Canyon Shuttle runs from 7:00 AM to 7:15 PM, with nine stops along the way. The shuttle takes approximately 45 minutes, one way from the visitor center to the last stop, Temple of Sinawava.

The other line is also trendy, also known as the Springdale Shuttle Line. It runs from 8:00 AM to 7:00 PM, with nine stops within Springdale. Buses run every 10-15 minutes. Visitors can pay the entrance park fee after deboarding at Stop 1, Zion Canyon Village, at the pedestrian park entrance.

Therefore, this shuttle is a lifesaver if you are outside the park and need help reaching the entrance. It provides a convenient option for visitors staying outside the park or for those who want to explore the town's many shops and restaurants. The shuttle bus rules prohibit eating, smoking, and no pets, ensuring a comfortable and safe ride for all passengers. Only capped water is allowed on board.

My piece of advice is solid: If you are planning a trip to Zion National Park, take advantage of the free shuttle service. It's there for a reason. And you would be saving so much time! It is a great way to explore the park without worrying about parking or traffic. I also always use it when I am staying in the park.

For those who need it, here are the shuttle times for both shuttle lines. You will still need to check these because they could eventually change:

Zion Canyon Shuttle Times	March - May	May - September	September- November	November
First morning shuttle: Zion Visitor Center - Temple of Sinawava	7 AM	6 AM	7 AM	7 AM
Last evening shuttle: Temple	7 PM	8.15 PM	7.15 PM	6.15 PM

of Sinawava - Zion Visitor Center				

Springdale Shuttle Times	March - May	May - September	September- November	November
First morning shuttle: Majestic View Lodge - Zion Village	8 AM	7 AM	8 AM	8 AM
Last evening shuttle: Zion Village - Majestic View Lodge	7 PM	8 PM	7 PM	6 PM

I am also here to show you a Zion National Park and Springdale shuttle stops list. These are the stops for Zion National Park Shuttle:

1. Visitor Center

Nearest sites/trailheads: South Campground, Watchman Trail, Zion Visitor Center, Pa'rus Trail

Distance from the entrance: 0 mi

2. Museum – Zion Human History Museum

Nearest sites/trailheads: Pa'rus Trail

Distance from the entrance: 1 mi

3. Canyon Junction

Nearest sites/trailheads: Pa'rus Trail

Distance from the entrance: 1.7 mi

4. Court of the Patriarchs

Nearest sites/trailheads: Sand Bench Trail, Court of the Patriarchs viewpoint

Distance from the entrance: 3.2 mi

5. Zion Lodge

Nearest sites/trailheads: Zion National Park Lodge, Emerald Pools Trails, Red Rock Grill, Caste Dome Cafe

Distance from the entrance: 4.3 mi

6. The Grotto

Nearest sites/trailheads: Grotto Picnic Area, Grotto Trail, Angels Landing Trailhead, Kayenta Trail

Distance from the entrance: 4.9 mi

7. Weeping Rock

Nearest sites/trailheads: Weeping Rock Trail, Observation Point Trail, Hidden Canyon Trail, Echo Canyon

Distance from the entrance: 6.4 mi

8. Big Bend

Nearest sites/trailheads: Big Bend viewpoint, Virgin River Trail

Distance from the entrance: 6.6 mi

9. Temple of Sinawava

Nearest sites/trailheads: Temple of Sinawava, Riverside Walk, The Virgin River Narrows

Distance from the entrance: 7.7 mi

Below are the stops for the Springdale Shuttle Line:

1. Zion Canyon Village

Distance to Visitor Center: >0.2 mi

2. Cafe Soleil/Cliffrose Lodge Thai Sapa

Distance to Visitor Center: 0.2 mi

3. Whiptail Grill, Flanigan's Inn

Distance to Visitor Center: 0.4 mi

4. Desert Pearl Inn

Canyon Ranch Motel

Distance to Visitor Center: 0.8 mi

5. Bumbleberry Inn

Zion Pizza & Noodle Company

Distance to Visitor Center: 1 mi

6. Hampton Inn, Holiday Inn Express Bit & Spur

Distance to Visitor Center: 1.4 mi

7. Driftwood Lodge

Quality Inn & Suites-Montclair

Distance to Visitor Center: 1.8 mi

8. Silver Bear Enterprises

Park House Cafe

Distance to Visitor Center: 2.3 mi

9. Majestic View Lodge

Distance to Visitor Center: 2.8 mi

Conclusion

We've come to an end about how you can get around Zion National Park. Be it your own car, motorbike, walking or taking advantage of the shuttle lines. You be the judge.

Thank you for parking responsibly and helping preserve Zion National Park's natural beauty for future generations to enjoy! I want to make your visit to Zion National Park as pleasant as possible, so here are a few takeaways regarding parking and leaving your car.

If you wish to avoid delays or are in a hurry, I recommend parking in Springdale. Although parking in town is not free, paying for a hassle-free visit to Zion is a small price. Please note that the parking fee is separate from the park entrance fee.

FAMILY-FRIENDLY TRAILS

Finally, we have reached the section that talks about my favorite pastime but also shows you the goal of this book! Now that we are finally here, it is time to discuss hiking and whether these trails are for everyone since Zion National Park might not show off an aura of achievability to most beginners.

I remember back in the day when I was starting out hiking myself. Everything seemed like a challenge, but once you overcome it - You see how easy it has been all along. It just seemed like a problem for you then.

I understand that you might be feeling the same way yourself! This section here is to help you and your family overcome this. It doesn't matter if this is your first time hiking or if you are an experienced hiker taking the family out for an outdoorsy day.

All that matters is that you are together and that you are outside. Therefore, prepare yourself and your family because you will soon be hitting these trails.

Now, let's remember to talk about their trials too. What are they like, who can try them, and what can you expect? It isn't just for beginners; it is for the experienced ones needing a pick-me-up or reminder.

Therefore, family-friendly trails are a variety of hiking trails suitable for families with children of all ages. Why are they so popular, not just amongst families but amongst beginner hikers too? These trails are well-marked, relatively easy, and typically range from one to four miles in length.

In other words, they are short and accommodating to everyone. And in most cases, everyone can hike them! Still, you do need some preparation. That is why you need to do some research ahead of time.

This way, you will find a trail suitable for your family's fitness level and hiking experience. Make sure you know the trail's track, markings, and trailhead. Still, not all of it is done with research.

It may all sound exciting and new but hold your horses. You do need to take care of your safety first. That means the right gear and preparations. Even if this all sounds extra easy to you, you need to know some basics if you are a beginner.

Make sure to bring appropriate gear for all of your family members. That includes comfortable hiking shoes, lightweight layers, a hat, sunscreen, snacks, and plenty of water. Remember, you must be prepared for everything; your gear will help you in this mission.

Your safety is your responsibility, and your family's safety comes too! That is why you must bring a first aid kit, a whistle, and a charged cell phone. You may also want to get a map, compass, or GPS device to help you navigate the trail in case you lose your phone, or its battery runs out.

Still, let that not scare you! Hiking with your family should be a fun and rewarding experience. You are still here to have fun, not run up a mountain with your kids on your back. Taking breaks as needed, enjoying the scenery, and taking plenty of photos is what I do.

So, which hiking trail should you choose? How can you choose it with little experience? I know this all sounds so confusing. Worry not. I am still here.

If you're new to hiking as a family, don't be scared, and don't show your dislike. This way, your kids won't copy your feelings off of you. Start with shorter, more accessible trails and gradually work your way up to more challenging hikes.

This is more than just a tip for those that have a limited amount of endurance. If you do so, you will gradually fall in love. It will help build your family's confidence and endurance over time and make you return for more.

Hiking With Your Family in Zion National Park

Now, let's get to the point. These introductions might sound too long, but beginners must learn the basics. And I will have to cover them!

I am finally here, in Zion National Park, ready for a great experience with my family. What should I do? Before you head out on any hike, make sure you've planned ahead.

First of all, talk to your family members. Be there for them, answer their questions, and help them with their worries. It will deepen your bond and also give them a love of hiking. Check the weather forecast, trail conditions, and park alerts together. We must address a side note here; obtain any necessary permits or reservations for your hike.

Then, you will need to make a choice. There are numerous hiking trails in Zion National Park, and if you have more days for hiking, you can choose a few. These hikes range from easy to strenuous. Choose a hike that is suitable for your family!

After that, you will have to make sure to bring appropriate hiking gear. You can pack them together and choose the outfits as a whole. Still, you will need some basics or essentials like sturdy hiking boots, a hat, sunscreen, and plenty of water.

As I like to pack with my girls, I want to remind myself that the weather in Zion can be unpredictable. Bringing a lightweight jacket or rain poncho is always a good idea. I also pack it for each member of my family!

Now comes the repetitive but extra important part: Leave no trace. As with any outdoor activity, practicing Leave No Trace principles is essential. Please pack all your trash, stay on designated trails, and avoid disturbing wildlife. These are the ten commandments for every hiker, and while obeying them, you ensure a quality experience for everyone inside the park (not just yourself).

Last but not least, I will also remind you that Zion National Park is a protected wilderness area. Please respect the environment in every way you can! You can do so by staying on designated trails and living harmoniously with nature. Remember, we are all here because of her!

Whether you're hiking through a national park, a state park, or a local nature park doesn't matter. Short family-friendly trails offer a great way to connect with nature and each other. Next, we will discuss some quality family trails you can try in Zion National Park. Therefore, stay tuned!

Riverside Walk Trail

Permit: No

Length: 2.2 mi

Duration: 1-2 hours

Elevation gain: 57 ft

Fitness level: Easy

Seasons: All year

Trailhead: Temple of Sinawava

Shuttle stop: 9. Temple of Sinawava

Restrooms: Yes

Water filling stations: Yes

Wheelchair accessible: Yes

Pets: No

Trail Description

The Riverside Walk Trail was previously known as the "Gateway to the Narrows." Sounds boring, doesn't it? This easy hike sure deserved a new name that sets it apart because this beauty is unforgettable. Today we know it as "Riverside Walk," which makes it more family-friendly and appealing to visitors.

If you are starting out with hiking in Zion National Park, this is the number one trail you need to take. It is a flat, paved trail. Is there a better way to celebrate Zion in all its glory than inside its biggest canyon? The trail is perfect for everyone. With approximately 2.2 miles round trip, this trail is suitable for hikers of all ages and abilities.

After the trailhead, you will follow the paved road up the canyon. You don't need a permit for this section, and the whole hike will mostly take up to 2 hours, considering it is only 2.2 mi in length. What's best about it? You can hike here all year round!

The fact that there is only minimal elevation gain, a paved road, and it is wheelchair accessible makes it even more beautiful. Can you imagine the beauty? For every beginner, this is a must-see! The trail offers stunning views of the canyon walls and opportunities to see wildlife.

The hike follows the Virgin River through a narrow canyon that feels sacred and imposing, making it an immersive and unique experience.

As you hike, you will also enjoy the vegetation, including ferns, trees, and moss, that thrive on the moisture supplied by the weeping walls. Can you imagine how much water this area gets, considering it is in the middle of the desert?

Are you into wildlife or bird spotting? This is the place to be, then! Riverside Walk is a great place to spot wildlife. You can see mule deer, blue herons fishing in the river, and squirrels and chipmunks begging for food. That is also why you can't bring pets along on this hike.

Take your time and enjoy the hike. This especially goes if you are with your loved ones. Remember, it's more about the journey than the destination.

Even if it is steaming hot, there is still stuff to do here on the Virgin River. In fact, several spots along the trail provide easy access to the Virgin River. That is if you want to cool off on a hot day.

Once you enjoy all of this beauty, it's time to finish up. Yes, the trail end is near. It ends at a point where the canyon is so narrow that there are no banks of land. That means the trail can't go on either side of the river.

This entrance also marks the beginning of the more rugged Zion Narrows hike. It is one of the most popular Zion hikes out there. Still, it is only for some, especially those coming unprepared. That is why most hikers tend to play in the water a bit and turn back.

In summary, this easy hike that has so much beauty, wildlife, and wild river to show off is perfect for families. I recommend it because it's a great way to experience the beauty of Zion National Park and connect with nature.

Trailhead Descriptions/Directions

Now, this one is easy! The Riverside Walk Trailhead is located at the Temple of Sinawava. To get to the trailhead, take the park shuttle to the Temple of Sinawava shuttle stop. It is the last stop on the Zion Canyon Shuttle route or stop number 9. In other words, regardless of whether you board the shuttle in Springdale or Zion, take the shuttle to the last stop and get out there.

The trailhead for the Riverside Walk Trail is located at the end of the paved Riverside Walk pathway. You can find it easily. Just look to the other side of the restrooms. In addition to these amenities, there is a large parking area at the Temple of Sinawava.

Therefore, don't panic because the trailhead is well-marked and easy to find. Apart from the trailhead offering hikers restrooms and water fountains, you can also find parking spaces and picnic tables here.

Highlights

What are the highlights of this trip? Apart from the beautiful Virgin River Canyon, I think one could also enjoy the wildlife here. There are numerous hanging gardens on the canyon walls, where wildflowers and other indigenous species grow.

You can bathe in the river, or reaching it is easy. Also, you can enjoy the other views outside the canyon, like The Altar and The Pulpit. Several informational signs along the trail provide information about the area's geology, flora, and fauna.

Things To Keep in Mind

You're choosing this trail to add to your itinerary? Well, lucky you. Now, what do you bring, and what information could help you? To make the most of your visit to the Riverside Walk Trail, arriving early in the day is a good idea.

That is if you want to avoid crowds. This especially goes if you are accessing the trail with a wheelchair or a stroller.

Like any other trail in Zion, you must bring plenty of water and sunscreen. Remember that the trail can be crowded during peak season. Refrain from being agitated by people and be prepared to share the trail with other hikers.

The outdoors belongs to all of us! Finally, be sure to follow all park regulations. These rules include not walking on unmarked trails, not feeding wildlife, not displacing, or drawing on rocks, and helping others.

Recommended Gear

Once this hike hits the plan, you will need some minimal (but essential) gear. This is the gear list I would recommend for Riverside Walk:

- Sturdy shoes
- Water shoes and neoprene socks if you plan on going into the water
- Hat
- Sunblock

Weeping Rock Trail

Permit: No

Length: 0.4 mi

Duration: 30 - 45 min

Elevation gain: 98 ft

Fitness level: Easy

Seasons: All year

Trailhead: Weeping Rock

Shuttle stop: 7. Weeping Rock

Restrooms: Yes

Water filling stations: Yes

Wheelchair accessible: Yes

Pets: No

Trail Description

Weeping Rock is a family-friendly hiking trail. This trail is a short and easy hike, making it a great option for families with children or those new to hiking.

Short but sweet goes the saying: trust me, this is true in Zion. If you have little time on your hands but want to see as much as possible, this is the trail for you. The Weeping Rock trail is approximately 0.4 miles long and takes 30 to 45 minutes to complete.

Even if you are a wheelchair user or need to take a stroller with you, it will work. It features a gradual incline of 98 ft and a paved pathway, making it accessible to everyone. Still, do expect some incline.

But why do I love it? It's short, offers amazing shade in the summer, and anyone can enjoy it. Hikers can enjoy stunning views of the surrounding canyon and lush hanging gardens along the way.

After crossing the bridge over the stream, the .06 mi paved trail will be open. You can visit it all year round but be cautious in winter due to the ice.

At the end of the trail, hikers will find the Weeping Rock. What is this? I first thought it was just a cool name. It is a large alcove with water dripping from the ceiling. The water seeps through the porous sandstone and forms droplets that appear to be weeping from the rock.

I know this sight sure is popular, especially in the summer months. This unique geological feature is a popular attraction in Zion National Park. Most people visit it as a spot for taking photos or enjoying a peaceful moment in nature. I use it to get away from the heat in the summer months.

Truth be said, most people use it for this too. It really can get crowded, especially for families with small children. Visiting early in the morning or late afternoon is best to avoid crowds.

Overall, the Weeping Rock trail is an easy and enjoyable hike. I jump onto it every time I visit since it offers stunning views and a cool breeze. It's an excellent option for families that want to cool down or learn something new through the experience.

Trailhead Descriptions/Directions

It's actually very easy to get to the Weeping Rock trailhead. If you are going with the shuttle from Springdale or Zion Canyon Visitor Center, you can't miss it. Depending on your location, the shuttle will drive 1.4 miles from Springdale to the park's south entrance.

After you board the Zion Canyon Line Shuttle, you will take the shuttle to Weeping Rock, stop number 7, and you should get off there. You will also find toilets and water filling stations here.

You can also reach the trailhead in winter if you are using your car. You can follow the same directions to the south entrance of the park. Then, drive another 1.5 miles to the Zion Canyon Scenic Route. Once you reach it, you will have to drive another 4.6 miles up the Scenic Drive until you see the Weeping Rock shuttle stop on your right.

This is where your drive ends. Finally, continue walking to the Weeping Rock trailhead. Where is it? After you park, look for a bridge. The trailhead is the bridge; once you cross it, the paved trail will be the Weeping Rock trail.

Highlights

What are the highlights? It's hard to tell because I love this straightforward and cooling trail (especially in the summer). Along the way, hikers can look for small trailside exhibits, where they will learn more about their surroundings. I love that the trail is mostly paved, making it a relatively easy hike.

One of the numerous highlights of the trail is the lush hanging gardens. Due to the continued moisture and water dripping from the walls and canyons above, these gardens have enough water and sun to thrive.

That is why the trail is so popular. It provides water and forms a unique oasis in the desert landscape. While walking this trail, hikers can enjoy a fantastic view of the Great White Throne. Truly, this view makes it look like a throne.

Things To Keep in Mind

Before going to the Weeping Rock trail, I want to share some important things to remember. Your safety and your family's well-being are in your hands. They are your responsibility, so make sure you have everything planned.

First of all, portions of the trail may be closed in the winter due to falling ice. Therefore, check with park officials before heading out. I love checking up with the rangers and asking about trail status every day before heading out.

Spring and Fall are the best times to visit if you want to see the most water flow. During the summer, the trail can be very crowded. That is why my family and I try to arrive early in the day or later in the afternoon.

Another thing I fully recommend is using the steps by the hiker's bridge. This way, you will have almost private access to the stream below. This area is very popular with children, and I use it as a fun way to cool off on a hot day.

In addition to the previous tips, it's important to note that the Weeping Rock trail is family-friendly, but dogs are not allowed on the course. The reason behind this is not just the steeper sections but also because it gets crowded, and dogs will get nervous.

Hikers should also be prepared to get a little wet! As you might expect, water flows directly out of the mountain face, dripping onto you!

Despite this being a short trail, it is moderately steep. You heard me right! You will get that exercise, all right. All hikers should be prepared for some uphill sections. There are water fill stations, but they may be turned off during the winter months.

Recommended Gear

Hikers should bring plenty of water, sunscreen, and sturdy footwear, as the trail can be hot and rocky in some sections. This is due to the water fountains occasionally being closed off and the desert sun reaching our skin. Due to the steep terrain, you might also want to have walking poles apart from sturdy footwear.

Therefore, the list of gear you might need for Weeping Rock Trail includes the following:

- Water
- Sunblock
- Hat
- Walking poles
- Sturdy footwear

Pa'rus Trail

Permit: No

Length: 3.5 mi

Duration: 2 hours

Elevation gain: 50 ft

Fitness level: Easy

Seasons: All year

Trailhead: Across South Entrance or Across Museum

Shuttle stop: 1. Zion Visitor Center 2. Human History Museum

Restrooms: Yes

Water filling stations: Yes

Wheelchair accessible: Yes

Pets: Yes

Trail Description

Now, this is one of those basic hikes you can do while walking to your trailhead. That is why it is so popular and visited! The Pa'rus Trail in Zion National Park is a 3.5-mile paved trail. It is ideal for those looking for an easy hike with almost no elevation change.

Why is it so popular? It is also wheelchair accessible, but some may need assistance. To reach it with a wheelchair, you can follow the path from the Human History Museum. Is there another reason for its popularity? Yes, this trail is unique as it is the only trail in the park that accepts pets and bikers.

In most cases, restrooms and water-filling stations are available at the Visitor Center. As you begin the trail, you will head north along the west bank of the Virgin River. It will truly be a beautiful sight to behold.

You will also see the Southern Campground, making it a great place to stay. After leaving the campground boundary, you will be surrounded by nature. While several spots give access to the river below, obey any "do not hike here" signs.

It's not all just straight from here. One point of interest is an old diversion dam that was used to shut the water to the town of Springdale. A sign explains this landmark's history and purpose, meaning there will soon be more signs to read.

Truly, you are sure to enjoy the part of the trail once you pass the museum. As the trail heads north, it zig-zags over the river several times. It winds like this until the end of the trail. At the northern end of the trail, visitors will pass under Route 9. This is a quick way to reach the Canyon Junction shuttle stop and to either continue their journey or head back.

I know it might sound boring, but the views here are truly breathtaking! Overall, the Pa'rus Trail may not offer dramatic scenery, but it is an excellent option for a leisurely stroll. If you ask me, adding your bike or pet is a bonus and a reason to visit.

Trailhead Descriptions/Directions

One of the most accessible trails to find is this one, and since it is also an amazing and long hike, you will see why it is listed here. You can use your car or enter the park with the free shuttle to reach the trailhead.

The trailhead will be easily reachable from three directions: From stop 1, the Visitor Center near the south entrance of the park; stop 2, the Zion Human History Museum; or you can get onto the trail from its exit at stop 3, Canyon Junction.

To reach it via car, drive to the entrance and enter the park, then choose which trailhead works for you and park there.

From the Visitor Center, cross the bridge on the Virgin River. You will see a campground, that is South Campground and cross the road to it. The trailhead should be right there.

Highlights

The Pa'rus Trail offers stunning views of the Watchman and follows the Virgin River, offering peaceful and picturesque spots to relax and enjoy the scenery. The name "Pa'rus" means "bubbling water" in the Paiute language, which is fitting as the trail passes several spots where the river creates small rapids and pools. The paved trail connects the Zion Canyon Visitor Center and Canyon Junction, making it a convenient and accessible way to explore the park.

Things To Keep in Mind

Remember, you are not alone on the trail, and please be open to sharing. You can bring your pets, but they must be on a leash, and remember to clean up after them. Bicycles are allowed but give way to pedestrians.

Like most hikes here, the trail can be busy during peak season. Therefore, be polite to other hikers, bikers, and pets. There are no restrooms or water-filling stations along the trail.

Still, you must avoid hiking mid-afternoon on hot summer days. For those taking the shuttle back to the Visitor Center in the late afternoon, consider getting off at the Canyon Junction and walking the trail back instead. Bikers will find this to be a preferred route over driving down the road to Canyon Junction.

Recommended Gear

This trail, while it might be longer, is relatively easy. That is also why you can freely bring minimal gear, but also be prepared in terms of sun protection and clothes. This is why I recommend:

- Sturdy footwear (Optional)
- Map
- Cap
- Sunblock
- Water

Lower Emerald Pool Trail

Permit: No

Length: 1.2 mi

Duration: 1 hour

Elevation gain: 69 ft

Fitness level: Easy

Seasons: All year

Trailhead: Across Zion Lodge

Shuttle stop: 5. Zion Lodge

Restrooms: Yes

Water filling stations: Yes

Wheelchair accessible: Yes

Pets: No

Trail Description

If you are staying in Zion Lodge or anywhere in the park, for that matter, this trail is a must-see for you. Apart from being right across Zion Lodge's entrance, it can also be combined with other trails. In fact, I really love this trail because it is a perfect cool-off for hot summer days.

Now, let's get to the point and discuss what makes this trail so high quality. The Lower Emerald Pool Trail is a popular hiking trail suitable for people of all ages and fitness levels.

As I might have foreshadowed so far, the trailhead for this hike is at the Zion Lodge. To get there, you can cross the footbridge and go to the north along the Virgin River. That is precisely why the trail is so popular, because of its serenity and beauty, but we are just at the trailhead.

In less than half a mile, the vegetation will become lusher. The first and more gardens start to appear. It is because the trail makes its way along the base of a tall alcove. Soon, it will wind around and be under two tall waterfalls.

It is known as Lower Emerald Pools. That is where the trails here get their names.

Still, the pools and their waterfalls are only sometimes there. It's important to note that these waterfalls are mostly seasonal. In other words, you might come along one summer and be surprised not to see any pools.

The waterfalls often flow strongly during spring runoff or after recent rainstorms. That is when you are sure to see them. Sadly, they may be down to a trickle during the drier summer months or fully disappear. That is when you might go on this hike but not see anything. Still, the hike is worth it.

Now, what makes this hike so popular? It's easy to get to this point, even if you're elderly or pushing a baby stroller. In other words, it is a wheelchair-accessible hike. It is 1.2 miles long and takes about an hour to complete. The trail is mostly flat, with an elevation gain of only 69 feet.

It's a great trail to do with family or friends, and even for those not into nature. There are restrooms and water-filling stations along the way, but pets are not allowed on the trail.

This hike connects to the Kayenta, Middle, and Upper Emerald Pools trails for a longer, moderate hike. Please note that swimming is prohibited in the Emerald Pools since wildlife uses these pools for water sources.

Trailhead Descriptions/Directions

Another easy-to-reach trailhead is this one. It is a popular hike, not just because of its beauty but because it is so close to Zion Lodge. If you are reaching the trail on foot, use the free Zion Shuttle. After the entrance, you should get off the shuttle at Zion Lodge or stop number 5.

One will reach the trail after they cross the highway bridge and follow the path along the Virgin River. This way, you can enjoy the trail regardless of where you are coming from, whether Zion Lodge or Springdale.

Because the trailhead is right across the highway to Zion Lodge, full services are available. You can find restrooms, water-filling stations, a snack bar, and a restaurant, making it an excellent hike right before lunchtime.

Highlights

Now, once you've read all of this, can you imagine how beautiful this hike is? Apart from being swamped with people in the summer due to its location, I totally recommend it.

The highlights of Lower Emerald Pools Trail include the beautiful pools and waterfalls, which you can see mostly in Spring. What sets them apart is also the easy connection to other trails like Kayenta, Middle, and Upper Emerald Pools trails, meaning that this can be a loop trail too.

As said before, its location across from Zion Lodge and its length of 1.2 miles are also a highlight, making them perfect for every family. It's an excellent trail for a short, easy hike with beautiful views. I am sure you will enjoy the lush vegetation and water features.

Things To Keep in Mind

I really hope you chose this trail to add to your trip plan. That goes not just for summer but also in the mid-season and winter too. In any case, there are a few things you need to know before going on this trail.

As you may have learned, you should remember that swimming in the Emerald Pools is not allowed. It is a protected area reserved only for wildlife. Depending on the water height, the waterfalls may flow less during summer.

Stay on designated trails to avoid getting lost or injured, even when the trail is crowded. Wildlife may approach visitors looking for food but feeding them is prohibited and can be harmful to their health.

As mentioned before, always bring plenty of water, especially during the hot summer months. You can also use the water-filling stations and restrooms available at the Zion Lodge. You won't be able to find any along the trail, so plan accordingly. Also, pets are not allowed on the Lower Emerald Pool Trail, so leaving your furry friends home is best.

Recommended Gear

This hike might sound short, but it does have a lot of runoff water, and the fact that it connects with other trails is an extra incentive to bring along some gear. These are the essentials, so don't forget to take the following:

- Water
- Sunblock
- Hat

- Walking poles
- Sturdy footwear

Conclusion

After we have covered my favorite short hikes of Zion National Park, it is time to do a brief recap. This national park is excellent for families looking for short and easy hikes, as you might have seen so far. They all offer beautiful sceneries and unique experiences inside canyons and near wildlife. However, visitors should know the potential hazards and take appropriate precautions. That is why I recommend wearing sturdy footwear, bringing plenty of water, and staying on designated trails.

Stay tuned to learn more about other medium and more demanding hikes which you can also do with your family. That is, if these three were too short and easy for you!

MODERATE TRAILS

O h, you should have seen the joy we found once we transitioned from day hikes that last two hours to actual hiking. It was like we found ourselves, my husband and I, and my girls. We were all so happy.

I used to prepare for these hikes all week by planning and brainstorming. Today, it takes much less time. And I hope for you too. That is why I am writing this ideal list of the best moderate hikes in Zion Park.

I am sure you will feel the same joy we did but remember to ease into it and not rush anything. Let us first cover what these moderate hikes are like.

As the name suggests, they have a moderate level of difficulty and typically require a moderate level of physical fitness. It does not mean that an out-of-shape person can't engage in hiking them. On the contrary, it would be wise to enjoy some easy hikes and proceed only with moderate ones. But I am sure these hikes are for all able-minded people.

These trails can vary in length, terrain, and elevation gain, but they generally have some steeper sections. While they might sound scary, some may require scrambling over rocks or other obstacles. That does not mean you can't do it. You just never tried it.

But what makes these hikes so popular, and why is everyone eager to take part in them? Because they offer amazing views and give you time for yourself! A moderate hiking trail can typically take anywhere from 1 to 4 hours to complete. That all depends on the length and elevation gain.

Therefore, not every trail is made equal. But the same goes for hikers too! Still, there are some factors that can make a trail moderate. They include the overall length of the trail, the amount of elevation gain, the trail's steepness, and the trail's terrain.

If one trail is accessible in all but one perimeter, the trail is still considered moderate. Therefore, do not underestimate hikes! Trails with some uphill sections but not too steep are often considered moderate. As I said, it is always different. Similarly, trails with some rocky or uneven terrain but relatively easy to navigate are also often considered moderate.

Still, all of it depends on us. For me, a moderate trail is different compared to a beginner's moderate trail. It's important to remember that what is considered moderate can vary depending on an individual's fitness level, experience, and personal preferences.

What Rules to Follow When Hiking Moderate Trails?

Apart from the preparations you need to take while hiking with the family, the trail has some unwritten (and sometimes written) rules.

Why do I follow these, and do I believe they matter? All these rules are here because other, more experienced people and I, with numerous years of hiking under my belt, have thought of them. I believe in these because they make a world of difference.

This goes for the rules that count on the trail and between the group. Here are the rules I recommend while hiking medium hikes with your loved ones or friends:

- Always stay on designated hiking trails! Off-trail hiking can lead to soil erosion, trampled vegetation, and the destruction of habitats.

- The slowest person needs to be on the head. It is an excellent recommendation because it lets you stay together while still having fun. None of your friends will ever feel left out again!

- Remember to pack out all of your trash. That includes food wrappers, tissues, and any other garbage you may generate on the trail.

- Keep a safe distance from wildlife and avoid feeding them at all costs. Feeding wildlife can cause more damage than good. It will also cause them to become habituated to humans, which is dangerous for both humans and animals.

- Drink up! Bring plenty of water and encourage everyone in your family to drink regularly. This goes for those, even if they don't feel thirsty.

In the end, remember that it's all about the group. Short trails can be an excellent way for families to enjoy the outdoors. The goal is to spend time together while experiencing the beauty of nature.

Moderate Hikes in Zion National Park

Now that we have covered what kind of trails we are expecting and which rules to follow while hiking them, it is time to address these types of hikes in Zion! Yes, there are many of them, and in this section, we will cover a few of them.

Moderate hikes in Zion National Park offer a good balance of challenge and enjoyment. Just as most of us like them. Nature, landscapes, and easy (but not too easy) hikes. As you might have learned so far, these hikes usually involve some elevation gain but are manageable.

Perfect for even beginners if you ask me. Still, like most hikes, they may have some rocky or uneven terrain but are generally well-maintained and easy to follow. These types of fun hikes may take several hours to complete but usually do not require advanced hiking skills or equipment.

What makes them the best? Because, as said before, almost anyone can do them. They are suitable for most moderately fit individuals and can be a great way to experience the beautiful scenery of Zion National Park. Finally, let us talk about some trails. Stay tuned if you want to know more about a few moderate hikes in Zion National Park.

Emerald Pools Trail

Permit: No

Length: 3.2 mi

Duration: 2.5 hours

Elevation gain: 350 ft

Fitness level: Middle

Seasons: All year

Trailhead: Across Zion Lodge

Shuttle stop: 5. Zion Lodge

Restrooms: Yes

Water filling stations: Yes

Wheelchair accessible: No

Pets: No

Trail Description

You might be thinking right now: Didn't we already talk about this trail? Well, I did tell you before about the Lower Emerald Pools trail, which is a great beginner and easy hike.

Now, if you really love this trail or want to explore it further, there are possibilities. You can revisit the Lower Pool or take the whole trail yourself. In any case, whatever you decide, it will be a good decision.

This trail covers three pools with unique emerald colors, perfect for a summer hike to hide from the sun. Therefore, it is time to read and learn about this recommended trail. The Lower, Middle and Upper Emerald Pools Trail in Zion National Park is a 3-mile hike. For a medium trail, it is pretty straightforward.

You will enjoy this hike due to an elevation change of 350 feet. From start to end, it takes about 2 and a half hours to complete. The trail entrance is the same as the Lower Emerald Pools trail, beginning at shuttle stop number 5 Zion Lodge. Still, it is not an easy trail since it isn't wheelchair and stroller accessible and has an uneven surface of sand and rock.

The trail becomes more challenging after the Lower Emerald Pool. Nothing to worry about still since it goes up the slopes and around some interesting boulders. Kids will enjoy this section, but still, be sure you have your gear, so no accidents occur. The goal is to lead you to the top of the cliff, which you can see from the Lower Pool.

The Middle Emerald Pools are created by two streams, surrounded by stunning scenery. If you love waterfalls, this is the place since you can see two here. Finally, the hike to Upper Emerald Pool is the most strenuous part of the trail. This is a sandy final quarter mile, especially in the hot summer sun. This is why I recommend bringing enough water and sun protection.

However, it is worth it if you decide to take the Upper Emerald Pools trail to reach the final pool. It lies at the base of the 300-foot cliffs above, and believe me, this hike is so worth it. The upper pool area is a lovely, shaded spot to enjoy your lunch in. Here, you will see the waterfall coming from the Heaps Canyon above.

I know it might be tempting, but it is important to note that bathing and walking through the pools is not allowed. On the other hand, you can enjoy the lush vegetation and the sound of the waterfall.

Overall, the Middle and Upper Emerald Pools Trail is a moderately challenging hike. I love it, including many other hikers, because it offers rewarding views and experiences. To return, you can either go back the way you came or take the western loop back to the Lodge.

Trailhead Descriptions/Directions

Getting here is easy. Park or get off the shuttle near the Zion Lodge or stop 5. If you're not sure how to get there, take the shuttle to Stop 5, exit to your right, and follow signs to The Emerald Pools Trailhead.

To get there via car, drive 1.5 miles from the park entrance and turn left at the sign for Zion Lodge and Scenic Drive. Drive 2.7 miles up the Scenic Drive and park at the small lot on the left across from The Zion Lodge.

Regardless of if you are getting here by car or shuttle, the trailhead to Lower Emerald Pools is the same. After crossing the parking lot across Zion Lodge, get to the footbridge on the Virgin River. You will need to cross this footbridge and follow the river. You can use restrooms and water filling stations here too.

Highlights

If you ask me, this is the ultimate summer trail. That is due to the numerous shaded areas you will encounter. Also, the numerous waterfalls, but there are more. The Middle and Upper Emerald Pools offer several highlights, including stunning waterfalls, beautiful alcoves, and natural pools.

At the end of the trail, you'll find yourself surrounded by colossal cliffs on three sides, creating a natural amphitheater. This is where the Upper Pool rests. You are sure to enjoy the majestic views of Zion Canyon from here.

Things To Keep in Mind

Still, while this hike might seem easy, there are quite a few things to keep in mind while hiking it. During the winter months, portions of the trail can be closed due to falling ice, so make sure to read these signs.

The best time to see waterfalls is during the Spring and Fall. However, the trail can be very crowded in the summer months, so starting early or later in the day is recommended to avoid the crowds. Also, the waterfalls are thin in summer and have much less water.

Never go inside the pools, and never feed the wildlife! It is also essential to keep an eye on your children, as there are drop-offs and steep cliffs along the trail. Both starting points have water fill stations and restrooms available.

Recommended Gear

This is not a beginner trail, so make sure you have all of your gear with you. First and foremost, make sure to wear good walking or hiking shoes. These will provide support and traction on uneven sand and rock surfaces.

I also recommend hiking poles, especially for those who may need additional balance or support on the trail. If you plan on hiking during the summer months, it's essential to bring a hat and sunblock to protect yourself from the weather.

Remember, with the right gear, you'll be able to enjoy the beauty fully, so bring these along:

- Sturdy shoes or hiking boots
- Hiking poles
- Hat
- Sunblock
- Water

Watchman Trail

Permit: No

Length: 3.3 mi

Duration: 2 hours

Elevation gain: 368 ft

Fitness level: Middle

Seasons: All year

Trailhead: Behind Zion Visitor Center

Shuttle stop: 1. Zion Visitor Center

Restrooms: Yes

Water filling stations: Yes

Wheelchair accessible: No

Pets: No

Trail Description

If it is raining on one of the days you plan on visiting Zion National Park, or if you have a few hours to kill but don't want to wander off too much, I think I have a great idea for you. This is the Watchman Trail, a perfect medium hike for those that only have a little time or want to stay out of the hustle and bustle.

It is a moderately challenging hike with an elevation change of 368 feet and over a distance of 3.3 miles. In most cases, it takes about 2 hours to complete. You can take this trail throughout the year and use restrooms and water-filling stations at the Visitor Center.

The beginning of the trail isn't as exhilarating as it follows the river and goes behind some employee housing. But bear with me. It gets much more exciting! Soon, things get more picturesque as the trail becomes more challenging. That includes climbing uphill and looping around a small valley. It is a beautiful sight if you visit it in the summer, perfect for families and picnics.

After passing the valley, you will see your first cliffs above the main canyon, where things become more interesting! As the trail turns back west, hikers will reach a charming viewpoint.

From here, you will see the Virgin River, Visitor Center below, Springdale in the distance, and the impressive Watchman Peak to the south.

This hike isn't so popular, but this viewpoint is an excellent spot to take a break and have lunch. That isn't all! A short loop trail that provides more views to the south has been added. After this, you can hike back to the Visitor Center.

Trailhead Descriptions/Directions

The trailhead is located at shuttle stop #1, the Visitor Center. To start the Watchman Trail, walk towards the main Route 9 road from the Zion Visitor Center. Look for the trailhead sign on the north side of the road. It should be on the east bank of the Virgin River. Here, you can also find restrooms and water-filling stations before you begin your hike.

Highlights

While the hike may not seem like much at the beginning, it gets much more elevated and beautiful soon into the hike. This trail provides a scenic viewpoint and panoramic views of Zion Canyon, including the Visitor Center complex, Springdale, and the stunning Watchman Peak.

Once you are there, the viewpoint is a great place to relax and enjoy lunch while taking in the stunning scenery. One of my favorite advantages of this hike is that it is less crowded than many of the more popular trails in Zion.

Things To Keep in Mind

Just like any other hike, this hike is no joke. It does have some elevation gain, and it takes work to scale. Still, it will all be worth it. Just make sure that you are safe.

The thing you need to have in mind if you choose to hike this breathtaking trail is that you may encounter some moderate drop-offs. This also means that you must stay alert while hiking and exercise caution. A thing I don't like about this hike is that during wet weather, the trail can become muddy and slippery. This is why I recommend wearing appropriate footwear.

Recommended Gear

Remember, your gear should help you while walking. That is why I want to ensure you have the proper footwear, hiking poles, and enough water. Bring a hat and sunblock to protect your skin if the weather is hot, especially since the trail has almost no shade. This is the gear I would recommend for this hike:

- Hiking boots
- Hiking poles
- Sunblock
- Hat
- Water

Canyon Overlook Trail

Permit: No

Length: 1 mi

Duration: 1 hour

Elevation gain: 163 ft

Fitness level: Middle

Seasons: All year

Trailhead: Zion-Mount Carmel Tunnel Entrance

Shuttle stop: No shuttle

Restrooms: Yes

Water filling stations: Yes

Wheelchair accessible: No

Pets: No

Trail Description

Is this trail right for you? Well, if you love a good landscape view and are okay with steep drop-offs on your trail sides, then it is. I love it because it offers a fantastic view of the canyon below, the scenic road, and the rest of the park.

This is one of the most memorable hikes here, so I definitely recommend it. This goes especially if you can't hike Angel's Landing for any reason imaginable. It is a short hike of only 1 mile. Due to the elevation gain, it takes around an hour to complete, with an elevation change of 163ft.

You need to know that it is not accessible by shuttle, so personal transportation is required. In other words, you do need your car to do this hike. The trail is located near the east entrance of the Zion-Mount Carmel Tunnel, and parking is minimal.

Now, you must be dying to know what this hike is like. Well, it can be challenging. After climbing up the Slickrock above the road, where the trailhead is, the manufactured trail takes hikers around the beautiful sandstone formations. You will go above the Pine Creek slot canyon, with railings in place for many sections of the trail. Therefore, don't worry about your balance, but still be cautious.

Halfway to the viewpoint, the trail enters a shaded alcove, perfect for those summer months. It has ferns growing out of the sandstone walls, providing a great shade. Soon, you will be able to reach the viewpoint.

Once at the viewpoint, a plaque identifies prominent landmarks. You can see Route 9 switchbacks below, Bridge Mountain, the East Temple, and the Pine Creek stream far below. While this might sound short, it is worth the elevation and height. The trail itself consists of long drop-offs and can be rocky and uneven at times. Let that not scare you. You are sure to enjoy the breathtaking views of the canyon!

Trailhead Descriptions/Directions

You cannot reach this trailhead with a shuttle, only with a private vehicle. You will need to drive up Route 9 to the upper-east entrance of the Zion-Mount Carmel Tunnel. This is where you will park but be warned that parking is minimal. If parking is full, keep driving down and you should see several overflow parking lots. As you might expect, the small parking lot on the south side of the road fills up quickly during the busy summer months.

Once you get a parking spot, the trailhead is relatively easy to find. The trailhead is located behind the ranger traffic booth on the north side of the road. This is where you will start your journey.

Highlights

I love this hike; its major highlight is the breathtaking views you can enjoy here. This hike offers stunning views of the towering red cliffs, deep canyons, and unique rock formations that Zion National Park is famous for. If you are looking for a shorter, less crowded hike in Zion, this is the one. Along the way, hikers can see the Route 9 switchbacks below. But that is not all. You will see Bridge Mountain, the East Temple, and the Pine Creek stream far below from the viewpoint.

Things To Keep in Mind

While the hike is truly beautiful, it does come with some warnings. When hiking the Canyon Overlook Trail, it is vital to keep in mind that there are some exposed spots. This is also where a fall could be dangerous.

Therefore, when hiking, be careful with children or anyone who may need more support on their feet. When hiking this trail, I, too, exercise extreme caution. Because cliff edges are everywhere, falling from the viewpoint could be fatal.

Recommended Gear

This trail is no joke, so ensure you have all your hiking essentials. You will have to wear proper walking or hiking shoes as the trail consists of uneven rock surfaces requiring support and traction. I always bring hiking poles, and this goes especially for those who need additional balance or support. These are the items I always bring:

- Sturdy shoes or hiking boots
- Hiking poles
- Hat
- Sunblock
- Water

Conclusion

Zion National Park offers a plethora of medium hikes for visitors to enjoy. These hikes allow one to experience the park's stunning natural beauty while being accessible to most hikers.

This is why we need to respect mother nature and never underestimate her. Therefore, it's always a good idea to research a trail we plan on taking. We need to understand its difficulty level before attempting it. Things such as bringing appropriate gear and supplies for the hike are key elements that we should take seriously.

THRILL SEEKING HIKES

I know that most people probably won't even look at this section and these hikes. They will just scroll to the end or only read the headers. I'm glad you are not one of them because look at you - You're reading the longer hikes section.

Regardless of if you want to enjoy reading about Zion National Park or if you want to keep yourself educated hike-wise, I am glad you are here. Let us talk about the more thrill-seeking hikes that offer amazing views.

I understand that most of us are scared of these hikes, probably because we think we can't do them. Well, I'm here to help you and tell you, you can do these hikes! Don't trust me? Read on!

Please don't shy away from this section of our book! These hikes might sound too harsh, especially if you're a beginner and don't have that much stamina or believe they are too tough for your whole family.

I thought so, too, when I started hiking with my family. The extreme or longer hikes were not something for me. On the contrary, these hikes are for everyone. Even if you don't reach the peak or your goal, these hikes are fantastic for building your stamina, self-reliance, and hiking ability. And yes, this even goes for the whole family.

The fact that they could see something so extraordinary or enjoy the view will keep them hooked on hiking. The same would go for you, even if your goal still needed to be reached!

Therefore, I want to remind you that not each hike aims to reach a peak or a point. On the contrary, every hike, regardless of length, elevation gain, or anything else, is there to help you enjoy nature and see it in all its forms.

Therefore, let us enjoy nature and ravish the fantastic landscapes of any national park or nature herself. I will now tell you about the different types of hikes with longer durations and higher elevation gain. You will learn what it means to be an expert hiker and what these hikes are like, but I also recommend trying or at least reading about them to know what experts are like.

Expert hiking trails are designed for experienced hikers who are physically fit and have a good endurance level. Unlike beginner and short hikes, these trails are often more challenging than regular trails. What most of us don't think of is that they also require a greater level of skill and experience to complete.

In a nutshell, they are typically longer, steeper, and more rugged. Here you are sure to see uneven terrain and will have to manage difficult obstacles. Believe me, I have tried it, and it feels miserable at first, but when you do it, it feels incredible. So, if you're still uncomfortable with these obstacles, wait it out.

Needless to say, while they are challenging, they offer stunning views and unique experiences. Believe me. These are popular choices for seasoned hikers!

But are there any other differences between these hikes and other hikes? Yes, in fact, the level of difficulty and the physical and mental demands are the most significant differences. If you are not ready for this, wait it out. These trails often require more than the basic high physical fitness and endurance level. They look for various technical skills you need to become more familiar with.

What most of us need to think of are these details. The other side is quite scary since these trails may also involve risks such as weather conditions, dangerous wildlife, or remote locations.

I am sure you are asking yourself if you can even attempt these. Well, these hikes have manageable sections in most cases but know that expert trails are unsuitable for beginners. That also goes for those with limited hiking experience.

This sounds unfair. Doesn't it? You do need to know that they require proper planning and preparation. That means appropriate gear and equipment, which you might have yet to have. Even if you get it at an outfitter, you might need to learn how to use it. Knowing your limits and hiking with a partner or group is also vital for safety.

Thank you for taking the time to read about expert hikes, even if you want to avoid engaging in them! Still, be warned that these hikes are strenuous and that some people and some families might not be fit enough for them.

On the other hand, that does not mean they can't try them and turn around once it gets too harsh for them. I recommend knowing yourself first, trying some light hikes, seeing how your family and your body act, and only then trying medium and expert or thrill-seeking hikes.

Thrill Seeking Hikes in Zion National Park

You can find all types of hikes here in Zion National Park! As you might remember, we already covered easy walks or beginner-friendly hikes, perfect for every family regardless of the children's ages. We also covered some medium hikes, suitable for couples and families that already know how to hike together and groups of all kinds.

Next, we have longer thrill-seeking and more expert hikes that require more elevation gain. These hikes are strenuous, no children's game, but they are also extremely rewarding in terms of views and mental positivity.

As you might have expected, Zion National Park offers a variety of hikes that cater to thrill-seekers and experienced hikers. Like anywhere else in the world, these hikes are typically characterized by steep inclines, narrow paths, and exposure to heights or drop-offs. What makes Zion hikes so unique is that some of these hikes require technical skills such as climbing, rappelling, or canyoneering.

Since there is so much to explore, there are many expert hikes in Zion National Park. These attract more than just experienced hikers who are up for a challenge but inexperienced ones who ask for guides' help.

Needless to say, these are still not for everyone, even if you have a guide. They are not for the faint of heart and require high physical fitness and technical skills. And why are there so many expert hikes here? There are so many thrill-seeking hikes in Zion National Park due to its unique geography and geology.

I've said it a million times, but I will say it again: The breathtaking beauty! The area is home to towering cliffs, narrow canyons, and breathtaking landscapes. Since this is so, you might expect many of these hikes to offer unparalleled views. It is really so, and they all make the strenuous journey well worth the effort. That even goes for those seeking an adrenaline rush.

There are so many wild hikes because the park itself is full of wilderness. More than half of its area is covered in wilderness areas, also known as backcountry. These hikes might be more challenging for some people because they are out of reach of phone reception, have no internet, often scarce water, and almost no electricity.

These hikes are meant for seasoned hikers who know how to use their water supply with no electricity and how to act when there's wildlife near them. However, it is important to note that these hikes can be dangerous! If you plan to undertake them, you will require proper preparation and caution to ensure a safe and enjoyable experience.

Therefore, before heading out on any of these thrill-seeking hikes, ensure you have a steady mindset, all the needed gear, and know how to act in the wild. All of this and knowing how to hike and navigate around borderline areas together with other hikers on the trail might be hard for most of us. But it is nothing new for experienced hikers and families that know what they're doing.

In the end, these expert hikes are still a step up from beginner and medium hikes, but they're possible to scale. Let us now look at the four most beautiful sections of Zion National Park that are all perfect for experienced hikers.

Angels Landing

Permit: Yes

Length: 5 mi

Duration: 4-5 hours

Elevation gain: 1,488 ft

Fitness level: Strenuous

Seasons: All year

Trailhead: The Grotto

Shuttle stop: 6. The Grotto

Restrooms: Yes

Water filling stations: Yes

Wheelchair accessible: No

Pets: No

Trail Description

Now comes one strenuous hiking trail which offers a breathtaking view. It is Angels Landing, a bucket-list hike all visitors need to try. It is one of the most popular hikes in Zion National Park and one of the most dangerous hikes in the United States.

This unique mountain formation lies in the center of Zion Canyon, visible from almost anywhere. The trail itself was constructed in the 1920s, following the narrow spine. It was so popular because of the amazing viewpoint 1,500 feet above the canyon floor. Even the first Europeans here thought of it as an amazing location, where angels land, and that is where the name comes from.

Needless to say, it is only for some. This trail is not recommended for individuals who have a fear of heights or balance issues. Most hikers believe it to be similar to Half Dome in Yosemite National Park. I believe so, too, because Angels Landing is a shorter yet strenuous hike. The difference is that it offers much more views.

It spans a total length of 5.4 miles and takes about 4 hours to complete. It depends on how crowded the trail gets; it can get super packed, especially in summer. The trail boasts an elevation change of 1488 feet, which can be challenging even for experienced hikers.

Therefore, ensure you have at least one hour extra to spare if you need rest. As I have said, I will repeat it: Visitors need a permit to access the trail. It is all part of the pilot permit program. Therefore, only attempt to hike the trail if you have a permit.

But how can you start when you don't even know where? Most hikers begin their journey at shuttle stop number 6, The Grotto. In most cases, visitors can only access the trail by shuttle. If shuttle services are closed during winter, hikers must drive to the trailhead themselves.

Now, let's look at the hike itself and see what this is like. The trail can be divided into five sections, each with its own unique features and challenges. The Grotto Trailhead is the starting point for most hikers. And from there, the trail winds through the Virgin River Valley.

Soon you will enter the second section, Refrigerator Canyon. This section is the only shaded part of the hike. Therefore, be prepared and enjoy the coolness if you are hiking in summer. If not, hurry through this section because it can get extra long.

Next follows the third section of the trail, known as Walter's Wiggles. This part of the trail includes 21 switchbacks that lead up to Scout Lookout. These are essential sections because, after about two miles, hikers will have already climbed 1,000 feet in elevation. That is a lot of elevation!

After you cover this, here comes the fourth section. The above-mentioned Scout Lookout is next. It is the turnaround point for those who may not be ready to continue to the top. Don't be sad! It was still worth it because the view is amazing. From Scout Lookout, hikers can enjoy panoramic views of Zion Canyon.

The trail's last section is where things get more challenging, but I am sure you will love it! Known as The Spine or Hogsback, this half-mile section includes steep drop-offs on both sides. And this is no game. The sides have 800-1,000 ft cliffs.

Let that not scare you away because you will be protected along the way. There are chains available for hikers to hold onto for extra safety. However, take your time since taking your time is crucial. Most hikers proceed carefully through this section. In most cases, it requires hikers to use both hands and feet to navigate the tricky terrain.

Finally, if you pass the Hogsback, you will reach the top of Angels Landing. Now, you can enjoy stunning views of Zion Canyon and the surrounding area. You have finally finished your bucket list hike. Celebrate!

It was all worth it because the Angels Landing trail is a challenging but rewarding hike. I know it was scary, and if you're unsure whether to add this hike to your plan, think again. Despite the challenge, many visitors are drawn to Angels Landing for its breathtaking views and unique hiking experience.

As you might have understood so far, the trail provides a thrilling adventure with an adrenaline rush, complete with steep drop-offs and narrow ridges! Overall, I recommend Angels Landing. It is a must-visit trail for those looking for a thrilling and unforgettable experience in Zion National Park.

Trailhead Descriptions/Directions

Reaching the trailhead is relatively easy. All you have to do is reach the first stop of the Zion Shuttle at the south entrance. From there, board the free shuttle and proceed with riding it until stop 6, The Grotto. The trailhead is located near the restrooms and the picnic area.

Visitors can also drive to the trailhead during the off-season when shuttle services are closed, but parking is limited and fills up quickly.

Highlights

This is the most fulfilling hike in Zion, landscape-wise. I am sure you will see some of the most spectacular views from here. From the summit, hikers can enjoy panoramic views of Zion Canyon and the surrounding red rock formations.

Another highlight for most hikers is the narrow and exposed route most of us enjoy. On top of that, the Angels Landing rock formation itself is a unique geological feature. As you might have seen, it is a narrow fin-like ridge. Most describe it as just out into the canyon, another fantastic thing to see.

Things To Keep in Mind

Remember, Angels Landing is a thrilling but dangerous hike! You will be hiking a narrow rock formation. This is why I would not recommend it for young children or those who have a fear of heights. Just like with other hikes, but this one in particular (due to its crowdedness), remember to share the trail with other hikers, allowing them to pass at safe spots. As with all hikes, please practice "leave no trace" ethics!

Due to its immense popularity, you might have read or heard that a permit system has been implemented. As of April 2022, you will need to obtain a permit to hike this trail, and the goal is to manage the crowds. You must apply for the seasonal lottery well in advance, or you can try to participate in the Day-Before lottery.

Also, be sure to check the weather before heading out, as the trail can be dangerous during rain or thunderstorms! Another thing to remember is that no bathrooms are on the trail. Therefore, if you need to use the bathroom, do so before heading out. If you need to, put solid human waste and toilet paper in a plastic bag and carry it back with you. Leaving human waste on the trail can result in a citation and a fine.

Recommended Gear

Before hiking the trail, make sure to download or print your permit and bring it with you! Rangers will be on site to verify if you have a permit or not. That is the most important addition, but wearing ankle-supported boots with good traction is also crucial. Remember, blisters and ankle injuries are common on this hike.

During winter hikes, it's a good idea to have microspikes for your shoes and gloves for the chains. These can help provide extra grip and warmth in snowy or icy conditions. Bring enough water, a sun hat, and sunblock during summer hikes. Here is the recommended gear I would take on this hike:

- Permit
- Boot
- Microspikes (for winter only)
- Water
- Sunblock
- Sun hat
- Hiking poles

Scout Lookout

Permit: No

Length: 3.6 mi

Duration: 2-3 hours

Elevation gain: 1,100 ft

Fitness level: Strenuous

Seasons: All year

Trailhead: The Grotto

Shuttle stop: 6. The Grotto

Restrooms: Yes

Water filling stations: Yes

Wheelchair accessible: No

Pets: No

Trail Description

Can't take the Angels Landing trail? Don't be bummed out! This is because an awe-inspiring trail called Scout Lookout is next to it. I recommend this trail to those with a fear of heights that can't hike Angels Landing for any possible reason or for those that don't have a permit to hike Angels Landing. I know Angels Landing is a great hike, but not all of us can hike it due to limited permits.

If you're one of those people who didn't get a permit the day before or throughout the season, even though you've tried a million times, this hike is perfect for you! It follows the same trail and has the same five sections, but you don't hike the final section of the Angels Landing peak.

So, what is this hike like? Scout Lookout Trail is a 3.6-mile roundtrip hike that provides stunning views of the surrounding landscapes. The trail has an elevation change of 1,100 ft and takes approximately 2 to 3 hours to complete.

As you might have understood before, Scout Lookout is the closest point hikers can get to Angels Landing without holding onto the chains and navigating the narrow and exposed rock formation.

Therefore, don't lose hope if you don't get your hiking permit. No, you can still hike the same trail. This goes even if you got a permit and still didn't want to or were too scared to hike the Angels Landing peak section.

Trailhead Descriptions/Directions

To reach the Scout Lookout trailhead, visitors will need to take the Zion Shuttle from the first stop or south entrance, then continue onto stop 6. During the off-season, visitors can drive to the trailhead but should remember that parking is limited and fills up quickly.

The trailhead is located near the picnic area and restrooms. The Grotto Trailhead, which is the starting point for the Angels Landing hike, lies here, at stop 6 for the Zion Canyon Shuttle.

Highlights

Just like Angels Landing, the highlights of Scout Lookout include amazing views. Much less than those all the way at Angels Landing, but still able to compete. In addition, you don't have to have a permit!

Things To Keep in Mind

While this hike might not be as strenuous as Angels Landing, there are still a few things to keep in mind. Remember to be considerate of other hikers, especially on crowded trails like this one. Before setting out on the trail, check the weather forecast to avoid dangerous conditions during rain or thunderstorms.

If you don't have a permit, please do not attempt to hike the Angels Landing trail. It is done with a permit for a reason. It's also important to note that there are no bathrooms on the trail, so be sure to take care of any needs before starting the hike.

Recommended Gear

I recommend hiking shoes, poles, and water for each hiker. In addition, during summer, I would also bring along a hat and sunblock due to exposure to the trail. Here is my list for the Scout Lookout trail:

- Hiking shoes

- Hiking poles

- Water

- Hat

- Sunblock

The Narrows

Permit: Yes, only if you are hiking The Narrows Top-Down

Length: 3-16 mi

Duration: 4 hours-All day

Elevation gain: Differs

Fitness level: Strenuous

Seasons: Summer- Autumn

Trailhead: Temple of Sinawava

Shuttle stop: 9. Temple of Sinawava

Restrooms: Yes

Water filling stations: Yes

Wheelchair accessible: No

Pets: No

Trail Description

Another hike I genuinely enjoy and recommend for those that really want to experience Zion National Park is The Narrows. The Narrows are the best hike that shows off what Zion and the Virgin River have to offer. You can follow the trail that goes from both river bottoms to the classic trail toward Mystery Canyon, but you will still have to be prepared to face this thrill-seeking hike.

One can definitely say this is a challenging and unique hiking experience in Zion National Park that mixes water and land. As you trek through the beautiful canyon, remember that there are a lot of people there and expect a slower pace. Nothing new here, is it?

The trail is busiest during the summer months, but Spring can be challenging due to snow melting and high water levels that can cause closures. There are multiple ways to hike this trail, which will surely be a memorable adventure.

The Narrows hike offers different options for visitors to explore this unique mixture of water and land trail. Here are a few options:

- Bottom-Up hike is the most popular and requires no permit, making it accessible to all visitors. It is undoubtedly the most popular and quite exhilarating. The trail spans 9.4 mi and starts at shuttle stop number 9, Temple of Sinawava. However, hikers can only go as far as Big Springs and back.

- Top-Down hike spans 16 mi and requires a permit, which can be difficult to obtain due to its popularity. The hike starts from Chamberlains Ranch and goes downstream to the Narrows one way. Hikers must arrange for a shuttle to get back to their starting point.

- The Wall Street hike is 7.5 mi long and does not require a permit. This hike takes visitors through the famous narrow section known as Wall Street.

- The Mystery Falls hike spans only 3 mi and does not require a permit. This short hike is perfect for those who want to experience the river and the stunning scenery of The Narrows but do not want to commit to a longer hike.

I mean, just imagine how beautiful it is to hike the Narrows. I remember it as one of my fondest memories in Zion National Park, hiking here with my daughters and husband and enjoying every moment of it.

Regardless of which route you choose; this hike is a must-see for those with the stamina. In the end, remember that this hike might be thrilling while combining river and land, but it is only for some. I recommend it only to those with the physical capability, stamina, and knowledge to navigate it.

Those that can't do this hike alone can try it with a guide, but those that don't have a guide and don't have the knowledge should definitely not attempt it. If you are in the last group, you can educate yourself or slowly build your way to hiking the Narrows.

Trailhead Descriptions/Directions

Now, this one is easy if you are like me. You should take the Zion Canyon Shuttle to reach the trailhead for The Narrows at Shuttle Stop 9, Temple of Sinawava. Ride the shuttle to its final stop. You can also drive to the trailhead, but parking is limited!

Once at the Temple of Sinawava, the trailhead is located at the end of the Riverside Walk. The trailhead is clearly marked. In other words, take the Riverside Walk trail from the Temple of Sinawava to reach the Narrows trailhead.

Highlights

Oh, the highlights. I don't know where to begin! The Narrows is known for its breathtaking views of towering cliffs, narrow canyons, and the Virgin River flowing through them. Truly, a hiker's paradise.

Most people enjoy that the hike involves wading through the Virgin River. That is what makes it a one-of-a-kind water hiking experience. In other words, you'll have to navigate the river, which can be anywhere from ankle-deep to waist deep.

Things To Keep in Mind

The Narrows can (theoretically) be hiked year-round, but each season has its pros and cons. In the summer, the water flow is low, making it easier to hike. As you might expect, visitors are higher in numbers. This is also when we need to be aware of flash floods, which occur during monsoon season.

During the fall, the water flow is at its lowest, and no special gear is required, making it a pleasant time to hike. I recommend this time for hiking but so do most other visitors.

However, the winter presents challenges due to higher water flow, so I recommend checking the data before going off. Of course, there is still the risk of hypothermia and falling ice during the colder part of the year. That is why you will need to wear a wetsuit or a dry suit. But that is not all. Neoprene socks and mittens or gloves might be good too.

In the Spring, the water flow is very high due to snowmelt, and visitors need to have the same gear as that in winter, with the possibility of trail closure due to high water.

Rest assured. You don't have to buy these for yourself. Rental gear is available in multiple rental shops in the surrounding areas. Zion Outfitters is one of them, located near the park entrance.

Just like the rest of the park, this hike can be quite busy during the summer months. Remember to check the weather forecast and water levels before heading out and be prepared!

Recommended Gear

If hiking during winter or early Spring, renting cold-weather gear from an outfitter in Springdale is highly recommended. These gear rentals can include trekking poles, canyoneering water boots, dry suits, and bibs to keep you warm.

Another thing to keep in mind when hiking The Narrows is the water temperature. Wearing neoprene socks is recommended as the water can be cooler, and neoprene wet socks will help keep your toes warm.

Additionally, it is vital to bring emergency gear, such as a flashlight and a set of dry layers, in a ziplock bag. If you are bringing your own gear, bring trekking poles or sticks for added support. It's essential to stay hydrated. Bring at least one liter of water, and even more during hot weather.

The Subway

Permit: Yes

Length: 8.2 mi

Duration: 5-9 hours

Elevation gain: 600 ft

Fitness level: Strenuous

Seasons: Summer- Autumn

Trailhead: Left Fork Trailhead

Shuttle stop: None

Restrooms: No

Water filling stations: No

Wheelchair accessible: No

Pets: No

Trail Description

Do you not want to hike where there are too many people? This hike is similar to The Narrows, only more intense. For most of the route the stream is the trail. This is an 8.2-mile hike up the Left Fork of North Creek to the Subway section. It is one of the most popular routes in the national park, and rightfully so.

On this hike, you can see many cascades, waterfalls, and the famous lower Subway formations, which take 5-9 hours and are a full day in remote scenery. There are two ways to hike it:

- Top-Bottom hike is the most popular. It is not for the faint of heart since it requires a lot of knowledge. It requires rappelling skills, 60 feet of rope, and experience.

- Bottom-Up is a great way to enjoy nature but it is also very hard to do.

Regardless of which way you choose, you'll be hiking along the banks, boulder-hopping, and hiking in the stream on this hike. Don't be worried. There are obvious trails along the banks.

Soon, you'll eventually have to hike in the stream. Don't try to avoid it; everyone gets their feet and legs wet on this hike. After two miles, the scenery becomes more beautiful, with solid rock and cascades. You'll see two 15-foot-tall waterfalls. Once the canyon makes a sharp turn to the right/south, you'll be able to see the dramatic lower Subway.

Finally, we reached our destination. It is a short section of the canyon where both walls come together, and the flowing water has cut out a hole. Here you will enjoy the flowing water in the emerald pools. This is a magical spot in the desert.

Once you reach the lower Subway, know this is the turnaround spot for this hike. Retrace your steps and hike back out when you're done. The hike out should seem more straightforward but remember to watch for the exit spot and allow plenty of time. Many tired hikers forget to watch for the exit, making it for a much longer, miserable hike.

Trailhead Descriptions/Directions

This trail has no shuttle, so you must use your vehicle to get here. Follow the Wildcat Trailhead located on Kolob Reservoir Road. It is about 15.3 miles above the town of Virgin. Once on the trail, follow the mostly level and well-maintained trail northeast for about half a mile from the parking lot.

Eventually, you will come across cliffs overlooking the Left Fork. Keep following the trail, which will take you down a steep descent of around 400 feet but remember this spot so that you can find your way back later.

Highlights

If you want to enjoy a hike with stunning views of cascades, waterfalls, and unique rock formations, this is the one for you. The highlight of the hike is the famous lower Subway section. This is where the canyon walls come together, creating a hole made from the water.

Things To Keep in Mind

As you might have heard, to hike through the Left Fork/Subway in Zion, you need a Wilderness permit from the National Park Service. The canyon is very popular, and they use an advanced lottery system to give out 80 permits a day. Will you be lucky enough to get one? Hope so!

Remember to keep an eye on the time and avoid being stuck in the Left Fork after dark. The best time to go is in Spring, Summer, or Fall, but it can be tricky in April because of spring runoff. If you go in winter, ensure you have enough protection from the cold water. Don't go if there's a chance of rain!

Needless to say, this hike is quite challenging. It will give you rough terrain, including a steep and loose slope, obstacles in the river, and slippery, wet rocks. It takes a while to complete, and you'll get wet, so plan accordingly. It's not an easy hike! You don't need special gear for canyoneering, luckily.

Recommended Gear

The Subway hike in Zion National Park can be challenging and requires proper gear that isn't so hard to come by. On the other hand, if you wish to hike the top-down section, you will need canyoneering gear (not listed). Here are some gear recommendations:

- Hiking shoes

- Hiking poles

- Water

Conclusion

For those adequately prepared and up for the challenge, these hikes offer breathtaking views, unique formations, and an unforgettable experience. All this is in the remote and beautiful scenery of Zion National Park.

Ultimately, these hikes are not for everyone, so I recommend that you research, train, and learn, and only then should you engage in attempting these trails! If you don't seem fit for it or are too scared, wait and attempt them another time.

CONCLUSION

The end of our journey is near, but as nature teaches us: Every end is a new beginning. Let this end be the beginning of your hiking journey!

So far, we have covered the history of Zion National Park, where we have explored both archaeology, geology, and modern history of what we know as Zion today or Mukuntuweap.

We have spoken about lodging options inside and outside the national park, how one can enter the park, park entrance fees, and acquiring permits for visiting protected areas. Then we covered the transportation options and understood that one can visit the park with their own car or via a free shuttle bus.

Last but not least, we have covered the hiking section of the national park, which was this book's primary goal. After covering numerous family-friendly trails, they still feature beautiful scenery even though they're pretty easy. Next came moderate trails, which are perfect for families that know what they're doing and non-beginner hikers. And last but not least were the thrill-seeking hikes, which are challenging trails that offer amazing views.

Remember that each hike is different; while one might be extra exciting for you and your family, the next might be boring or too challenging. That is why every hike needs preparation and research. Your family should be aware of your plans and be comfortable with them.

Last but not least, understanding and friendliness between your group is key. My point is that your goal isn't to reach a peak or a specific spot. No, your goal is to have fun and enjoy nature!

I have said it a million times and will repeat it as many times as you need me to: Back in the day, while I started hiking, it was tough to get the information we now have access to everywhere. Be it through the internet, through other hikers, or books. That is why I have written this book for you because I wanted you to have an easier way to reach the information I didn't have.

In fact, now that you have all the tools needed for hiking in Zion National Park, make sure not to waste them! Make sure to go out there, hike those trails, enjoy the park, and celebrate your victory with your family.

Use the information I have given you! Sorry to say goodbye, but I'm happy I have had an opportunity to help you reach your goal. I hope you use it!

LEAVE A REVIEW

In the end, if you have enjoyed my book, how I have written it, the information I gave you, and anything else for that matter, please don't hesitate to tell me. Please do so by contacting me or leaving a review of my book on Amazon!

RESOURCES

Clear Content Marketing (2018, Jun 15) The Six Sections of Zion: An Explanation, Zion National Park, https://zionnationalpark.com/kolob-terrace/section/

Nicolas Brulliard (2018, Mar 15) How Mukuntuweap National Monument Became One of the Nation's Most Popular Parks, NPCA https://www.npca.org/articles/1784-how-mukuntuweap-national-monument-became-one-of-the-nation-s-most-popular?s_src=g_grants_ads&gclid=Cj0KCQjww4-hBhCtARIsAC9gR3b8wFuVxzzrlbZzkIfuPb4cAjcou63-nBM9LdqY4mrFMFbDwumegaIaAlD2EALw_wcB

Rachael Smith (n.d.) Things to Do in Zion National Park, Visit Utah https://www.visitutah.com/Places-To-Go/Parks-Outdoors/Zion/Things-to-Do-in-Zion-National-Park

Stephen Hutcheson, Lisa Corcoran (1951) Zion National Park, Utah, National Park Service https://www.gutenberg.org/cache/epub/59867/pg59867-images.html

Zion Canyon Shuttle System (2023, Apr 16) National Parks Service https://www.nps.gov/zion/planyourvisit/zion-canyon-shuttle-system.htm

Zion Canyon Trail Descriptions (2023, Mar 13) National Parks Service

https://www.nps.gov/zion/planyourvisit/zion-canyon-trail-descriptions.htm

Zion National Park Travel Guide 2023 (n.d.) Authentik USA https://www.authentikusa.com/uploads/destination_sheets/US/en_US/optimized/43.pdf

Made in the USA
Columbia, SC
19 March 2025